1

Identifying needs

Despite the significant number of children with SEN, little is known about the overall pattern of their needs. Whether and how children's needs are identified and, in turn, met appears to be influenced by a number of factors, including their gender, ethnicity, family circumstances and where they are educated. Most resources are concentrated on children with statements, leaving little scope for wider preventative work.

The high number of children with SEN calls into question how well our system of education is serving children whose needs differ – to a greater or lesser extent – from their classmates'. The long-term goal of SEN policy should be to shift the balance of professional resources towards making education more accessible for all children.

What are special educational needs?

11 Schools in England and Wales currently identify one in five children (1.9 million) as having difficulty learning, such that they need some form of help in class. These children are said to have special educational needs. One child in thirty (275,000) is considered to need more support than their school can provide. For them, the LEA draws up a 'statement', which specifies their needs and the 'additional or different' provision to be made.[I]

12 Children's needs arise from a wide range of difficulties – cognitive, physical, sensory, communication and behavioural; individual children often have more than one type of need. The support they receive in school is as varied as their needs, ranging from tailored teaching approaches or special computer equipment to separate day or residential provision. Some require help from health or social services – from occasional speech and language therapy to around the clock healthcare.

13 SEN is a significant and growing area of public expenditure.[II] Local authorities in England and Wales spent £3.6 billion on SEN provision in 2001/02, representing 15 per cent of spending on schools (or the 'local schools budget').[III] Most SEN resources – 69 per cent – are focused on the small of minority children with statements.

14 Surprisingly little is known at a national level about the pattern of children's special educational needs. In England, there are no common definitions of need, so while LEAs may hold detailed information on the needs of pupils in their area, this cannot be aggregated. By contrast, authorities in Wales and Scotland are required to report how many children have statements (or 'records' in Scotland) by type of need. This reveals a broadly consistent profile **[Table 1]**. No data are available on the needs of the much larger group of children – 1.6 million in England and Wales – who have SEN but do not have a statement.[IV]

A changing picture

15 Many of the school and local authority staff interviewed during our research commented on the changing nature of children's needs and the pressures created locally in terms of demand for specialist provision. However a lack of robust research evidence makes it impossible to say definitively whether there have been actual increases or decreases; rather, these trends may largely reflect developments in medical and educational practice.[V]

I   DfES and WAG. In 2001, 22 per cent of pupils in England and 21 per cent in Wales were identified by their school as having SEN and just over 3 per cent had a statement.

II LEA spending on SEN increased by 11 per cent between 1999/2000 and 2001/02 (earlier data were collected on a different basis).

III CIPFA education estimates 2001/02. LEAs in Wales spent £202 million and in England, £3.4 billion. These figures do not include pupil-led (or 'AWPU') funding, so SEN spending may be higher than this.

IV DfES and WAG, 2001; figures relate to pupils in primary and secondary schools who were on 'SEN registers'.

V   See literature review, pages 1, 6 and 7 (on limitations of existing data).

Table 1

Children with statements or records of need, by type of need

Data from Wales and Scotland reveal a similar needs profile.

Type of need	Percentage of children with statements/records, by type of need	
	Wales	Scotland
Moderate learning difficulties; MLD and others	33%	34%
Specific learning difficulties	16%	16%
Emotional and behavioural difficulties (Wales); social and emotional difficulties (Scotland)	11%	4%
Severe learning difficulties; SLD and others	11%	5%
Speech and communication difficulties (Wales); language/communication disorder (Scotland)	8%	9%
Physical disabilities (Wales); physical or motor impairments (Scotland)	6%	8%
Autistic spectrum disorders	5%	9%
Profound and multiple learning difficulties; PMLD and others	4%	1%
Hearing impairment	3%	4%
Visual impairment	1%	3%
Other	2%	6%

Source: WAG and Scottish Executive, 2001

16 Our national survey of LEAs indicates, over the last five years:

- significant increases in the number of children with autistic spectrum disorders (perceived by four-fifths of respondents), with speech and communication difficulties (two-thirds of respondents), and with profound and multiple learning difficulties (one-third of respondents); and

- significant decreases in few categories of need, except moderate learning difficulties (one-quarter of respondents) and specific learning difficulties (one-fifth of respondents).

17 Data gathered by the Welsh Assembly Government over the same period confirm local authorities' perceptions of:

- a significant increase (124 per cent) in the proportion of children with statements for autistic spectrum disorders and for speech and communication difficulties (44 per cent);

- an increase of 10 per cent in the proportion of children with statements for profound and multiple learning difficulties;

- only a small increase (7 per cent) in the proportion of children with emotional and behavioural difficulties – less than was perceived by survey respondents; and

- a decrease in the proportion of children with statements for moderate learning difficulties (13 per cent).

18 Reliable data on children's needs is an essential prerequisite to effective planning:

- **at LEA level**, to ensure an appropriate range of provision, allowing the great majority of children to be educated in local mainstream schools;

- **among groups of LEAs and at a regional level**, to enable joint planning and investment to meet the needs of children with more unusual 'low incidence' needs; and

- **at a national level**, to inform spending priorities, workforce planning, teacher training and programmes of research.

19 The DfES is currently developing broad descriptions of the different types of SEN for use in the pupil level annual schools census (PLASC) from 2004. This represents a welcome step forward and has the potential to underpin sensitive forward planning.[I]

20 At a local level, **we recommend that LEAs should analyse the changing pattern of needs to inform their inclusion strategy** – helping them to plan for developments in the overall pattern of provision, central advisory and support services, professional development programmes and capital expenditure. We also recommend that **LEAs, health and social services should share information on children with complex needs**, to enable sensitive forward planning to support them through early years, primary and secondary education.

Identifying special educational needs

21 Our analysis suggests that some groups are more likely to be identified as having SEN – which in turn influences how their needs are met in school and often, how much additional support they receive.[II] However, the likelihood of getting a statement appears to be influenced by a range of factors, relating to the child, their family and the institutions responsible for their education.

Type of need

22 Children with needs associated with a physical difficulty tend to be identified earlier and more reliably. However, most needs are not 'clear cut': for a significant majority of special needs there are no medical tests and different professionals may reach differing conclusions as to the underlying cause for SEN.[III] This may have significant implications on the level of support offered to individual children.

When you have a 'label' it is easier to get a statement.

Mother of a child with Down Syndrome

[I] The DfES is also working with the DoH to establish a 'common language' taking account of the different definitions used by education, health and social services in relation to SEN, disability and learning difficulties.

[II] See also our first report, *Statutory Assessment and Statements of SEN: In Need of Review?*, paragraphs 51-55 **(Ref. 2)**.

[III] See literature review, pages 6 and 7.

Gender

23 Although some conditions are known to occur more commonly among the male population – for example, speech and language difficulties – data from Wales show that boys are more likely to have a statement than girls, across every type of need **[Exhibit 1]**. Data from Scotland show the same pattern (equivalent data are not collected in England). Academic research also indicates that referrals by teachers and other professionals are biased towards boys.[I] This could mean that:

- girls may be disadvantaged by not having their needs identified and appropriate action taken; and/or

- boys may be disadvantaged by having their needs emphasised and being 'labelled' unnecessarily.

We recommend that further research is carried out to investigate the significant gender differences in needs' identification and the implications for how children's needs are met in school.[II]

[I] See literature review, pages 22-23.

[II] There are also significant gender differences in the special school population [paragraphs 52] and in permanent exclusions [paragraphs 69-72].

Exhibit 1

Children with statements by gender and type of need (Wales, 2001)

Boys are more likely than girls to have a statement, across every type of need.

Number of pupils

■ Boys
■ Girls

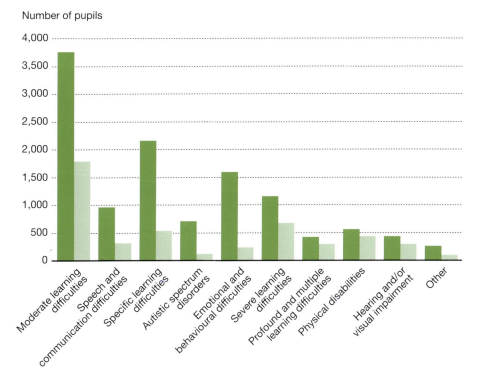

Source: *WAG, 2001; includes pupils in nursery, primary, secondary, special and independent schools.*

Ethnicity

24 The relationship between special educational needs and ethnicity is complex and the research evidence inconclusive.[I] Concerns raised during our research included:

- difficulties in accurately identifying SEN in children who are not fluent in English or who have only recently arrived in the country;

- inadequate translation and interpreting services, even in areas with significant minority populations; this was also an issue in Wales, for Welsh speakers;

- a lack of accessible information – for example, on statutory assessment – in minority languages, even in areas with significant minority populations; and

- a perceived stigma attached to SEN in some communities, manifest in comparatively low levels of identified need.

25 We asked parent-partnership officers (who provide impartial advice to parents on SEN matters) which parents they considered were 'hard to reach'. Minority ethnic groups and those who did not speak English as a first language were highlighted by almost two-thirds of respondents.

26 At present only a minority of LEAs collect data on the ethnic background of children with SEN: two-fifths indicated that they gather this information in relation to children with statements, and just over one-quarter for children with SEN without a statement. Only one in ten said that they made use of these data to investigate whether children from ethnic minorities were being over- or under-identified.[II] In future this information should become available through PLASC, which will include data on both the needs of individual pupils and on their ethnic background; **we recommend that the DfES and WAG should make this information available to LEAs to enable them to identify which groups are over- or under-represented.**

27 **We also recommend that LEAs should ensure that appropriate translation and interpreting facilities are available for children and parents whose first language is not English.** Collaboration with other departments, neighbouring LEAs, local agencies and community groups could help to make this cost-effective. In addition, Welsh LEAs are required to plan to provide bilingual services as part of their Welsh Language Schemes.

Family circumstances

28 Family circumstances also appear to influence whether and how a child's needs are identified – but again, the relationship is complex and varied.[III]

29 The link between the incidence of certain needs and socio-economic circumstances has long been known.[IV] However, we found only a very weak correlation between the incidence of SEN – whether measured by the proportion of children with statements or those with SEN without statements – and the level of deprivation in an LEA area.[V] This suggests that children from disadvantaged backgrounds are relatively less likely to be identified as having SEN, given their needs profile as a group. Conversely, our

I   See literature review, page 23.

II Audit Commission survey of LEAs.

III See literature review, pages 21 and 22.

IV Arguably the most significant study in this area was *Born to Fail?*, NCB 1973 **(Ref. 4)**.

V   Both analyses revealed a correlation coefficient of just over 0.2; deprivation ratings were drawn from the ODPM's Index of Multiple Deprivation.

research with parents suggests that those with the knowledge, resources and confidence to challenge staff in schools and LEAs are more likely to get their child's needs assessed and to secure a more generous package of provision.[I]

30 The emotional stability of the family is another important factor. Some of the files of children with statements for emotional and behavioural difficulties revealed traumatic home circumstances, including family breakdown, bereavement, domestic violence and abuse.[II]

School and LEA-related factors

31 There are significant variations in the proportion of children with statements between LEA areas and between schools, which call into question how far SEN reflects the real level of need among pupils, or rather, different institutions' ability to respond:

- the proportion of children with statements varies five-fold between LEAs in England and Wales; and

- the proportion of children with statements in schools varies greatly. For example, in England 15 per cent of primary schools have 3 per cent or more of pupils with statements compared with 36 per cent of secondary schools. And in Wales, 27 per cent of primary schools have 3 per cent or more of pupils with statements, compared with 55 per cent of secondary schools.[III]

32 This variation may be explained in part by local policy decisions, resulting in different eligibility criteria for statutory assessment, funding arrangements and so on. However, it also reflects varying attitudes and practice. Some highly inclusive schools have a lower level of statements than one would expect because they are more experienced at meeting children's needs and perhaps better equipped to do so. Conversely, some academically successful schools have a relatively high level of statements, given the needs of their pupils, because they have less experience of working with children with SEN.

33 Developing teachers' skills at recognising what is and what is not a special educational need could help to ensure a more consistent approach to identifying needs. New national standards for Qualified Teacher Status expect newly qualified teachers (NQTs) to: *'identify and support … those who are working below age-related expectations, those who are failing to achieve their potential in learning, and those who experience behavioural, emotional and social difficulties* **(Ref. 5)**. While this is welcome, it may be unrealistic to expect in-depth coverage of this during initial teacher training. **We therefore recommend that developing NQTs' skills and confidence at identifying SEN and making appropriate responses should be made a key element of the induction year.**[IV] Given the range of practice across schools, this might best be achieved by working in partnership with other local schools, both mainstream and special. The involvement of health and social services colleagues could also be valuable, although we acknowledge that resource constraints may inhibit such developments. These issues are discussed further in Chapter three [paragraphs 95-98].

I   See also *Statutory Assessment and Statements of SEN: In Need of Review?*, paragraph 55 **(Ref. 2)**.

II   Review of case files in fieldwork LEAs.

III DfES and WAG, 2001. See also *Statutory Assessment and Statements of SEN: In Need of Review*, paragraphs 51-54 **(Ref. 2)**.

IV   NQTs are required to complete a statutory induction period during their first year of teaching, intended to develop their skills and knowledge further. The TTA is currently reviewing the Induction Standards.

Early intervention

They helped me catch up with reading. I was at age seven when I got here, now I am on age 12, just a year behind. Mrs [SENCO] helped me a lot.

Secondary school pupil

34 Government policy in England and Wales emphasises the importance of early intervention. This is perhaps most immediately relevant to children whose needs may best be addressed by prompt action and support for a limited period. However, early intervention is also important for children with lifelong needs to ensure that they receive the necessary support as soon as possible.[I] Many of these children will be known to the health service long before they start their education, and effective information-sharing can help to ensure that their teachers are better prepared to meet their needs. But our interviews with headteachers and SENCOs suggested that often this required considerable 'chasing'.

35 In spite of a plethora of local initiatives, our research suggests that early intervention has yet to become the norm – in terms of age or level of need.[II]

36 **Arrangements for funding additional provision to meet children's SEN in the early years sector remain incoherent and piecemeal.** In the areas we visited, young children with higher levels of need were generally in special provision or had a tailored package of support. However, for other children with SEN, particularly those in non-maintained settings, there appeared to be little, if any, specialist advice, support or dedicated resources.[III] In most areas, the Early Years Development and Childcare Partnership (EYDCP) had identified a 'pot' from which providers could bid for funds to meet the needs of individual children – but success depended on knowing about the pot, putting together an effective bid and, crucially, the availability of funds.[IV] This situation should improve as a result of the new monies made available to establish a network of 'area specialists' and SENCOs across early years settings in England, but arrangements still fall far short of the level of advice and support provided for children of school age.[V]

37 **The older a child is, the more likely he or she is to have a statement.**[VI] This may reflect a variety of factors, including the widening learning gap between some children with SEN and their peers as they grow older; the general increase in behavioural difficulties at adolescence; and the organisation of secondary education, with larger schools, separate subject teachers and a demanding curriculum. Whatever the reasons, statements direct proportionately more SEN resources to secondary education than to primary, and more to primary than to nursery.

I   See also literature review, pages 15-17.

II Four-fifths of the LEAs responding to our national survey had local initiatives to improve early identification of children's needs.

III In England over one-third of three and four year olds are educated in private, voluntary or independent sector settings (36 per cent in Jan 2002). Data are not collected on this basis in Wales.

IV EYDCPs are convened by the LEA to oversee the planning and provision of local early education and childcare services; providers from all sectors are represented, as well as parents, employers and others. In England, a modest Specialist Support Grant is paid to EYDCPs to help support children with low incidence needs.

V   As yet there is no such initiative in Wales. Discussed in further detail in Chapter three, paragraphs 99-101.

VI Percentage of children with statements was in nursery – 1.3 per cent England, 1 per cent Wales; in primary – 1.7 per cent England, 2.2 per cent Wales; in secondary – 2.5 per cent England, 3.2 per cent Wales. DfES and WAG, 2001.

38 **LEAs' responsibilities towards children with statements may also be limiting their scope for investing in wider preventative work** with children with lower levels of need, at School Action and School Action Plus.[I] Over the last three years, LEAs in England and Wales increased their spending on children with statements almost ten times as much as they increased spending on children with SEN but without a statement.[II] Many LEA officers spoke of a 'catch-22' situation in this respect: their obligations towards children with statements meant that they were unable to spend more on children at School Action and School Action Plus; but until they did, demand for statements could be expected to continue to rise.

39 Action is needed on a number of fronts to make a reality of early intervention:

- **LEAs should seek to put in place, in partnership with local health and social services, systems for sharing information on young children with complex needs.**[III]

- **LEAs should review their arrangements for funding SEN provision in early years settings**, in consultation with the Early Years Development and Childcare Partnership. In particular, they should consider the availability of support and advice for children at Early Years Action and Early Years Action Plus and for children with SEN whose parents want them to attend a non-maintained setting.

- As LEAs are not currently funded for this purpose, we recommend that **Government should make available to LEAs funding to extend SEN advice and support to early years settings.**[IV] This could provide a more sustainable and cost effective way of developing specialist support for young children, building on recent initiatives to establish area specialists and SENCOs. It could also help to ensure the continuity of support on transition to primary school.

- **LEAs should, in agreement with local schools, set targets to shift the balance of specialist advice and support towards 'whole school' and 'whole class' approaches.** In other words, learning support services and the educational psychology service should spend more time advising teachers on effective strategies for responding to the diverse needs in today's classrooms, to ensure that good practice in working with individual children is embedded in school-wide policy and practice **[Case study 1, overleaf]**.[V]

I The Code of Practice sets out a graduated approach to meeting children's needs, involving action at three levels – School Action and School Action Plus and through statutory assessment, which in most cases leads to a statement being drawn up and additional help provided.

II Audit Commission analysis of CIPFA education estimates, 1999-2001. The average net increase in each LEA's spending on children with statements was £1.04 million compared with £0.11 million on children with SEN without a statement (in real terms, at 2001/02 prices).

III As per requirement to maintain a Register of Disabled Children, under the Children Act 1989.

IV At present, funding for children with SEN in early years settings is not identified within the LEA Standard Spending Assessment.

V See also paragraphs 78-79.

Case study 1
'Whole school' initiative to promote mental health – Slough

Slough LEA has been working in partnership with Slough Primary Care Trust (formerly Berkshire Health Authority) to promote a whole school approach to mental health – including whole staff training and preventative work with pupils. The project is funded by the PCT through their Partnership Development Fund.

A multi-disciplinary team was established to develop a range of materials and training for school staff, parents and pupils. Mental health awareness is promoted through:

- training workshops for 'whole school' staff groups and parents;
- 'circle time' workshops with pupils;
- advice on curriculum materials and resources that promote children's emotional well-being; and
- information on relevant services and organisations.

Feedback has been extremely positive. Young people have particularly valued the opportunity to discuss issues such as self-esteem, stress and anger, and to learn from each other. Staff have welcomed the whole school emphasis, raising awareness among all colleagues. The project targeted a number of secondary schools in its first year and is now being rolled out to all secondaries and piloted in primary schools.

Source: Audit Commission

2

Presence

While the number of children with statements in mainstream schools has grown, a significant proportion continue to be educated in special schools, some residential. The trend towards inclusion has been very gradual over the last two decades.

Although parents of children with SEN have the same right as others to express a preference for which school their child should attend, their choice is often limited by a lack of suitable provision locally and unwelcoming attitudes in some schools.

LEAs should seek to develop a spectrum of provision to ensure that, as far as possible, all children with SEN have the option of attending a local mainstream school.

Where are children with SEN educated?

40 Government policy over the last two decades has presumed children with SEN should be educated in mainstream schools, as far as possible. A parent's right to express a preference for a place in a mainstream school is clearly enshrined in legislation.[I] But how far is this achieved in practice?

I See Appendix 1 for further detail on the statutory framework.

II In England, the SEN Regional Partnerships are currently collecting data on children in residential schools; a DoH working group is also looking at this.

III PRUs provide education on a temporary basis for pupils who are unable to attend school, for a variety of reasons including exclusion. Permanent exclusions are discussed in Chapter three, paragraphs 69-76.

41 Most children with statements – approximately three-quarters in Wales and almost two-thirds in England – are now educated in the mainstream sector **[Exhibit 2]**. Meanwhile, a significant proportion continue to be educated in special schools, funded by the LEA to make appropriate provision for children with higher levels of need; and a small proportion in non-maintained and independent special schools, some of them residential. Nationally, it is not known how many children with SEN are being educated in residential schools or what their needs are.[II] Finally, a small proportion of children with statements are educated in pupil referral units (PRUs) and other out-of-school provision, often as a result of being excluded.[III]

Exhibit 2

Where children with statements are educated (2001)

Most children with statements are educated in mainstream schools.

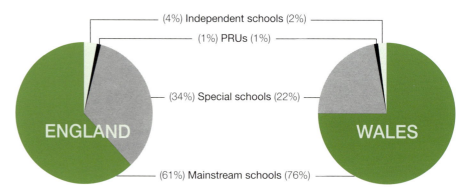

Source: DfES and WAG, 2001

Parental preference – getting into school

42 All parents have a right to express a preference about which school their child should attend and schools are legally required to admit a child if named in their statement.[I] However, the parents that we met tended to feel that they had little choice over which school their child could attend for one of two reasons:

- **There was no school or early years setting locally which they considered appropriate.** For example, several of the parents we met in Wales wanted their child to attend a Welsh-medium school, but specialist support was only available if they attended an English-medium school. And parents of children with autistic spectrum disorders in several areas complained of a lack of specialist expertise in relation to their child's needs. The limited availability of health and social care in mainstream schools was another factor often lying behind parents' decision to opt for a special school.

  I can sue the authority, but I can't put what I want in the schools.
  Mother of boy with autism

- **They felt that some schools and early years settings did not want their child to attend.** Several parents recounted how the schools they had visited had gently discouraged them from applying for a place, for example, by suggesting that another school might be more suitable.

  It took a whole year finding a school... one year for these kids is very precious.
  Mother

  They said they couldn't have him at school unless the LEA provided one-to-one support.
  Mother

  They don't say 'no' but they make their experience so unpleasant that they don't want to attend... it's not uncommon.
  SENCO commenting on school admissions

43 Their perceptions were confirmed by many of the headteachers, SENCOs and LEA officers we interviewed. Most headteachers were able to point to a local school that had a reputation for not taking children with particular needs and some admitted that they were reluctant to do so. Our questionnaire of 44 headteachers across five LEAs indicates that children with emotional and behavioural difficulties (EBD) are the group least likely to be admitted, by a considerable margin. Other groups frequently mentioned included children with autistic spectrum disorders, physical difficulties, and moderate or severe learning difficulties.

44 Our survey of parent-partnership officers paints a similar picture. They reported that those children most commonly experiencing difficulties with admissions were those who had been excluded, those with EBD and those with autistic spectrum disorders. Around two-thirds of respondents felt that children with physical difficulties and moderate learning difficulties experienced admission problems 'often' or 'occasionally' **[Exhibit 3, overleaf]**.

I   See Appendix 1 for further detail on the statutory framework.

Exhibit 3
Children experiencing difficulties with admissions
Children with behavioural difficulties have most problems getting into their parents' chosen school.

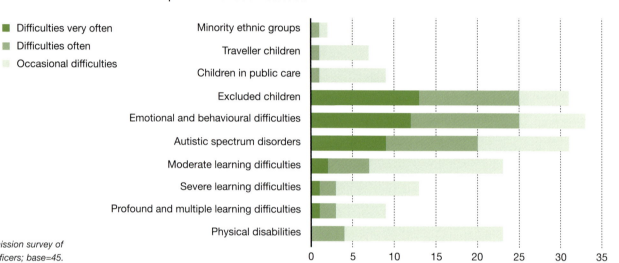

- ■ Difficulties very often
- ■ Difficulties often
- □ Occasional difficulties

Source: Audit Commission survey of parent-partnership officers; base=45.

45 While this suggests that some schools are less than willing to admit pupils with certain needs, it is also clear that others have placed great emphasis on developing an inclusive ethos. However, some such schools expressed concern about the 'magnet effect' created by their reputation and in some cases, by their specialist facilities. While there are benefits from having a 'critical mass' of children with particular needs attending a school, in terms of planning provision and developing staff expertise, there is also a risk that individual schools may become over-stretched and a polarised pattern of provision develop – restricting parental choice and effectively letting other schools off the hook.

46 LEAs should consider how they can help to make school admissions fairer for children with SEN. New regulations require LEAs to publish their arrangements for monitoring the admissions of children with SEN, both with and without statements **(Ref. 6)**. **We recommend that the pattern of admissions should be discussed at least annually by the Local Admissions Forum, with a view to encouraging a more even distribution of children with SEN. We also recommend that this should include a separate analysis of admissions for children with behavioural difficulties.**[I]

Trends towards 'inclusion'

47 Contrary to public perception, the move towards the inclusion of children with higher levels of need into mainstream education has progressed very slowly, with only a gradual reduction in the special school population over the last decade **[Exhibit 4]**.

I Local Admissions Forums involve the LEA, heads, governors and other interested parties. We acknowledge the constraints within which LEAs are working in seeking to influence school admissions.

Exhibit 4

Children in special schools in England and Wales, 1981-2001

The special school population has fallen very slowly over the last decade.

England
Wales

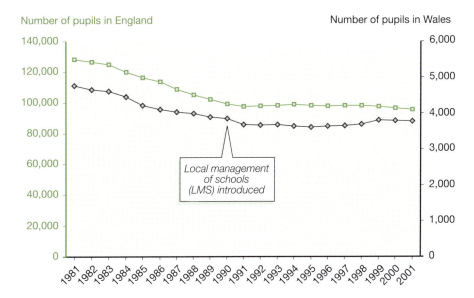

Number of pupils in England

Number of pupils in Wales

Local management
of schools
(LMS) introduced

Source: DfES and WAG; data relate to full and part-time pupils.

48 At the same time, there has been a significant blurring of the boundaries between the special and mainstream sectors. A spectrum of provision has developed ranging from:

- specially 'resourced provision' in mainstream schools typically involving specialist staff and equipment to support the inclusion of children with higher levels of need. In some areas, this has been done on a school-wide basis, in others, through the development of specialist classes or units. In Wales, 21 per cent of pupils with statements are currently in special classes or units in mainstream schools; equivalent data are not yet available for England.[I]

- dual registration arrangements, enabling pupils in special schools to spend part of the week in mainstream provision. In 2001, 2,330 children in England were dually registered; these data are not collected in Wales.

49 Such arrangements can help children with higher levels of need to reap the benefits of both sectors, in terms of specialist provision and increased opportunities to mix with their peers. They can also support the gradual transition of children from special to mainstream, allowing confidence to develop on all sides. There are however possible downsides. Children may feel that they belong on neither side and there may be practical difficulties such as travelling between sites. In addition, some question how inclusive such arrangements really are: children may be on site but the opportunity to spend time with their peers may be limited.

I WAG, 2001. The DfES is now collecting this data and expects to publish it in future.

Which children are educated in special schools?

50 Our research shows a number of trends in the profile of the special school population, in terms of pupils' age, gender and needs. However, it is first worth noting that the proportion of children in special schools varies more than tenfold across LEAs in England and Wales – from 0.17 to 2.29 per cent of pupils.[I] This reflects a combination of factors, including the historical pattern of provision and local commitment to enabling children with higher levels of need to be educated in mainstream schools.

Age

51 The special school population in England and Wales grows with each year group, with a leap around secondary transfer **[Exhibit 5]**. Parents, LEA officers and school staff commonly remarked that primary schools were more inclusive than secondary schools. This may in part reflect the organisation of secondary education – with its more formal curriculum, separate subject teachers and larger schools.

Gender

52 There are significant gender differences in the special school population. Sixty-eight per cent of pupils in special schools are boys.[II] This may reflect the fact that boys are over-represented among those with statements and in particular, among those with behavioural difficulties. However, it also raises questions about how effectively schools are responding to boys' needs.

I   DfES and WAG; data relate to children in special schools in 2000.

II DfES and WAG, 2001; data relate to pupils in maintained special schools, aged 2-19.

Exhibit 5

Age of pupils in special schools (England and Wales, 2001)

The number of children in special schools increases around secondary transfer.

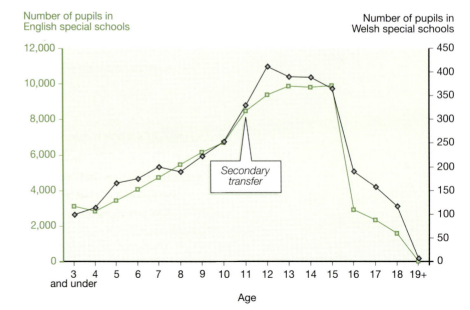

Number of pupils in English special schools

Number of pupils in Welsh special schools

- England
- Wales

Age

Source: DfES and WAG, 2001; data relate to full and part time pupils

A changing needs profile

53 Another trend often commented on was the changing needs profile of the special school population. Two themes were commonly raised:

- Special schools are educating proportionately more children with higher levels of need than they have historically, as children with lower levels of need are increasingly educated in mainstream schools. There also appears to be a growth in the number of children with profound and multiple learning difficulties.[I]

- Individual special schools are catering for children with a wider range of needs, as the number of special schools has fallen faster than the number of pupils educated in them.

54 The trend towards a special school population with increasingly higher level and diverse needs will make considerable demands on the skills of special school staff and on the facilities available to them. Moreover, given the historically slow pace towards inclusion, it seems likely that in most areas, special schools will continue to play a significant role in the spectrum of SEN provision, for the foreseeable future.[II]

LEA inclusion strategies

55 A key role for the LEA is to develop an inclusion strategy to ensure that all children's needs may be met locally and, as far as possible, in the mainstream sector.

- **The strategy should be 'needs-based'**, that is, based on an analysis of current pupils' needs and forward projections of the needs profile over the next five to ten years. In particular, LEAs should project the likely number of pupils with high support needs and take steps to enable them to be educated in local mainstream schools, as far as possible. Information from health and social services may be valuable in drawing up an accurate picture of this population.

- **The strategy should set out a timetable for developing the capacity of mainstream schools and early years settings to meet the needs of children currently educated in the special sector.** This will require active and ongoing consultation with schools and parents, a phased programme of capital investment, targeted professional development opportunities and careful planning of the role of central advisory and support services. Many children in special schools require health and social care, so it is critical to involve these services in transition planning.

- **The strategy should set out clearly the future role of special schools in the spectrum of provision** and how this is to be achieved. LEAs should consider:
  - the expected profile of the special school population and implications for training and capital developments;

[I] Many special school staff and LEA officers remarked on this trend; it is also consistent with the Welsh data discussed in paragraph 17.

[II] A Special Schools Working Group, reporting to the Ministerial working group on SEN in England, is currently considering the future role of special schools.

- promoting partnership working between mainstream and special schools (including non-maintained and independent schools), to make the most of specialist expertise and to create opportunities for children in special schools to spend time learning alongside their mainstream peers **[Case study 2]**; and

- in areas where a high proportion of children with statements are educated in special schools, LEAs should consider the scope for a further reduction in special school places, as children are increasingly included in mainstream schools.

56 An inclusion strategy will involve tough decisions and it is crucial that political leaders are fully engaged and committed. It will also require realistic financial planning and some important spending decisions. **LEAs should ensure that their inclusion strategy is consistent with all other aspects of strategic and financial planning: including their Accessibility Plan, Education Development Plan, School Organisation Plan, Asset Management Plan, Early Years Development and Childcare Plan, and, in Wales, their Welsh Education Scheme.**

Case study 2
Supporting the inclusion of children with severe learning difficulties in Herefordshire

Herefordshire LEA has for a long time included pupils with moderate learning difficulties in mainstream schools. In 1999 they initiated a programme to enable pupils with severe learning difficulties (SLD) to spend at least part of the week in their local mainstream school.

The programme involves all of the County's three special schools for children with SLD and so far, 29 mainstream schools. Staff suggest which children should be involved to the LEA's inclusion co-ordinator, who consults their parents and the mainstream schools near their home. Once a placement is agreed, the LEA employs a teaching assistant to support the pupil in their mainstream school, who spends time in both schools before the placement begins. The LEA also funds the child's teachers to visit each other's classroom, working together to develop an appropriate curriculum and targets. Staff training in 'Signalong' (a signing system for people with communications difficulties) has also been provided and where relevant, whole staff training on low incidence needs.

The programme has been running for three and a half years. Fifty per cent of pupils with SLD now spend part of the week in their local mainstream school. Strong links have been built up between schools and there have also been benefits for children outside the programme, as disability awareness, staff skills and confidence have grown. Recently mainstream classes have also begun to spend time in their classmate's special school.

Source: Audit Commission

SEN and Disability Tribunal

58 Parents have a right to appeal to the SEN and Disability Tribunal if they are not satisfied with the school named in their child's statement.[I] At present the majority (61 per cent) of Tribunal decisions supporting a change in the school named in a statement result in placements in special schools, mostly outside the maintained sector **[Table 2]**.[II] Only 30 per cent of such appeals in 2000/01 resulted in a place in a local mainstream school in the maintained sector. **We recommend to the SEN and Disability Tribunal that: it should reflect, in its annual report, on how far its decisions align with national policy on inclusion; and where, on the basis of the appeals it has heard, the key barriers to inclusion lie.**

Table 2
Tribunal decisions resulting in a change in school, 2000-01

Appeals resulting in placements in...

Mainstream schools		
Community	94	26%
Foundation	14	4%
Independent	31	9%
Total mainstream	**139**	**39%**
Special schools		
Community special	70	19%
Foundation special	5	1%
Non-maintained	29	8%
Independent	83	23%
Other	4	1%
Home tuition	29	8%
Total special	**220**	**61%**
Total – mainstream and special	**359**	**100%**

Source: Audit Commission analysis of data in SEN Tribunal Annual Report 2000/01. Appeals included are those which ordered the LEA to change the school named and all those which upheld part 4 of the statement.

I   Parents may also appeal about other aspects of provision in the statement, or if the LEA decides not to carry out a statutory assessment or not to issue a statement. See Appendix 1 for further detail on the statutory framework.

II   The President of the Tribunal has highlighted his concern that decisions based on an *'unrealistic assessment of cost could undermine the policy which favours including children with SEN in mainstream schools'* **(Ref. 7)**. This reflects a Court of Appeal decision which ruled that the cost of a place in a maintained special school should be taken as nil.

3

Participation

Although the majority of children with statements are educated in the mainstream sector, many continue to face barriers to learning, including:

- inaccessible buildings and facilities;
- shortfalls in specialist support; and
- exclusion from certain lessons or extra-curricular activities.

Disproportionately high levels of non-attendance and exclusion among children with SEN suggest that some are having a poor time. Action is needed at both a local and a national level to ensure that schools and early years settings have the necessary skills and resources to make inclusion work for today's young people, with their many and varied needs.

Accessibility

59 Schools have important new duties to plan strategically to increase their accessibility, in terms of their premises, curriculum and written materials.[I]

60 Physical access has improved in recent years, under the Schools Access Initiative in England. Between 1996 and 2002, £125 million was made available to improve the accessibility of school buildings. However, much remains to be done: in 2001, only 23 per cent of primary schools and 10 per cent of secondary schools were deemed to be fully accessible – ranging from 0 to 74 per cent of primary schools and 0 to 23 per cent of secondary schools, across different LEA areas. Washroom facilities and at least half of the teaching accommodation were accessible in only 14 per cent of primaries and 15 per cent of secondaries.[II]

61 There has been no such initiative in Wales and no data are available on the accessibility of Welsh schools. **We recommend that the Welsh Assembly Government evaluates the accessibility of school buildings in Wales and considers whether a dedicated funding stream – similar to the Schools Access Initiative – is needed.**

Access to all aspects of school life

62 Some children with SEN are regularly excluded from aspects of the curriculum, usually as a result of judgements made by teaching staff about the suitability of certain lessons.[III] For example, they may not attend foreign language lessons as it is assumed that they will not benefit from them, as was the case in one school we visited; or they may not be allowed into the science or technology laboratories because of fears about their safety. Such judgements tend to be rooted in genuine concern for their welfare; however, unless they are made openly and in consultation with the child and his or her parents, they may seem arbitrary and unfair – and could result in a child missing out inappropriately.

63 Concerns were also raised about the breadth of curriculum offered in some special schools, where a lack of subject expertise – and some suggested, low expectations – could result in fewer subjects being offered.[IV]

We can only teach maths and english GCSE here, because we only have five teachers in secondary.

Special school headteacher

64 Extra curricular activities – such as school trips, homework clubs and music – provide valuable learning opportunities for all children, as well as the chance to mix socially. However, there is much evidence to suggest that some children, particularly those with behavioural difficulties, are regularly excluded from such opportunities. Health and safety regulations were also given as a reason for sometimes not including children with physical disabilities. Less formally, several of the parents we met raised concerns about how far their child was accepted by his/her classmates and made to feel welcome in school.

I Further detail on the statutory framework is set out in Appendix 1.

II DfES, 2002 (Schools Access Initiative).

III See literature review, pages 26-28.

IV See literature review, page 26-28.

The minute he was naughty they banned him from everything!

Mother

He doesn't have dinner with the other children, he has it all by himself and is supervised by one other teacher.

Mother

He's not getting asked to birthday parties, not getting Christmas cards. It's painful for him, he's coming home crying his eyes out about it... Playtime's a problem.

Mother

65 The SEN Code of Practice **(Ref. 3)** clearly states that *'children with SEN should be offered full access to a broad, balanced and relevant education'* in England, *'including an appropriate curriculum for the foundation stage and National Curriculum'* and in Wales, *'based on the National Curriculum and for pre-school children, the Desirable Outcomes for Children's Learning Before Compulsory School Age'.* In addition, the Disability Discrimination Act places important new anti-discriminatory duties on schools – not to treat disabled pupils 'less favourably' than others and to make 'reasonable adjustments' to ensure that they are not disadvantaged.[I] We recommend that:

- **Schools should record decisions not to include a child in any aspect of school life (including extra-curricular activities) and report on this at their next review.**[II] This would enable such decisions to be discussed and reviewed with the pupil and his or her parents; and

- **where children with higher levels of need are joining a new school, their class teacher (or other staff member, as appropriate) should develop an induction programme.** Initiatives in place in some schools include advance visits to meet pupils and staff, setting up 'buddying' schemes and establishing a 'circle of friends' **[Case study 3]**.

Case study 3
Making children feel welcome at Bangabandhu School

Bangabandhu School is a community primary school in Tower Hamlets. Many of its pupils have SEN, some with significant disabilities. The school has a highly inclusive ethos and much care is taken to help children to settle in and make friends. A number of different approaches are used, including:

- establishing a 'circle of friends'. The SENCO – who has been trained in this technique – will ask a child who appears to be having difficulty making friends if they would like to try this approach. Classmates are invited to volunteer to be part of their circle, which will then meet weekly to plan how they will work and play together;

- carefully pairing pupils to read together – helping to increase their confidence and improve their reading. Older children who are struggling with reading have helped younger pupils to learn; and younger ones who are reading to a standard well above their age have worked with older pupils. Whole classes have also been carefully paired to read together; and

I   Further detail on the statutory framework is provided in Appendix A.

II Under the SEN Code of Practice, individual education plans must be reviewed at least twice a year, involving the parent and child where possible. Statements must be reviewed at least annually.

- encouraging classmates to welcome children whose physical or behavioural difficulties might otherwise set them apart. For example, when two children with complex needs were joining the school, future classmates volunteered to meet them in advance and then played an active role in helping them to settle in. In other cases, families have shared photos and teachers have explained to classmates that a child might look or act a bit differently, but that they should make an extra effort to make them feel welcome.

Source: Audit Commission

Attendance and exclusion

John did things because he knew he would get sent home, he thought the school didn't want him there. It was a lot quicker for them just to pick up the phone and call to us to pick him up.

Mother

66 Poor attendance and exclusion are indicators that things are not going well in school for individual children. There are clear links between these and long-term underachievement.[I] It is therefore of great concern that children with SEN are significantly over-represented in national non-attendance and exclusion statistics; indeed, our research indicates that the picture may be worse than these statistics suggest.

Non-attendance

67 Children in special schools have a higher rate of absenteeism – both authorised and unauthorised – than their mainstream counterparts **[Table 3]** and these levels have remained broadly constant over the last five years.[II] One explanation is the need to attend medical appointments, therapy sessions and so on; however this does not explain the higher rate of unauthorised absence – more than twice that of pupils in mainstream schools.

Table 3
Pupil absences from schools in England and Wales, 2001
Children in special schools are more likely to stay away from school.

Percentage half-days missed during 2000/01	authorised		unauthorised	
	England	**Wales**	**England**	**Wales**
Primary schools	5.6%	–	0.5%	–
Secondary schools	8.0%	8.9%	1.1%	1.6%
Special schools	**9.1%**	**11.7%**	**2.2%**	**3.2%**

Note: Welsh data on absences from primary schools not available.

Source: DfES and WAG, 2001

I For example, see SEU, *Bridging the Gap*, 1999 **(Ref. 8)**.

II Absence is 'authorised' if permission is given by a teacher or other staff member, for example due to illness or the need to attend a therapy session; and 'unauthorised' if this is not the case.

68   The pattern of absences for pupils with SEN in mainstream schools is unknown nationally and few LEAs are monitoring this. Less than one in five of the LEAs collect attendance data on children with statements and less than one in ten, on children with SEN without a statement. Of those who do, two-thirds reported that it had enabled them to target intervention and support to schools.[I] **We recommend that schools and, through them, LEAs should collect attendance data on all pupils with SEN, both with and without a statement.**

Exclusion from school

69   English data show that children with statements are three times more likely to be permanently excluded from school than other children. Although high, this represents a considerable improvement on previous years – in 1996/97, pupils with statements were eight times more likely to be excluded and in 1999/2000, seven times more likely. However, it is not known how far the improvement arises from recent changes in data collection methods.[II] Meanwhile, the latest data from Wales indicate that children with statements remain eight times more likely to be permanently excluded than their peers.[III] National statistics in England and Wales also demonstrate a consistently higher rate of permanent exclusions among pupils in special schools and a strong gender bias, boys account for almost nine-tenths of all permanent exclusions.[IV]

70   Unsurprisingly, pupils with emotional and behavioural difficulties are far more likely to be permanently excluded.[V] Little is known about the link between other needs and exclusions; less than one in five of the LEAs responding to our national survey said they collect data on permanent exclusions of children with statements by type of need. Such information could yield valuable insights into why children are excluded and enable strategies to be developed to reduce this. **We recommend that all LEAs collect data on permanent exclusions of pupils with statements, by type of need.**

71   No data are available nationally on the exclusion rate of the much larger group of children with SEN without a statement and fewer than one-half of authorities collect these data locally.[VI] Analysis of the data provided by 22 LEAs suggests that children with SEN (including those without statements) account for the vast majority of permanent exclusions – almost nine out of ten from primary schools and six out of ten from secondary schools **[Table 4]**.

72   If this pattern is replicated across other areas, it has important implications for national and local policy on school exclusion, suggesting that meeting children's SEN more effectively could result in a significant drop in the number of permanent exclusions. These figures also raise questions about:

- how far exclusions are the product of unmet special educational needs; and

- how far excluded children are receiving suitable provision to meet their special educational needs outside school. In addition, Ofsted **(Ref. 9)** recently highlighted a worrying trend towards *'extended placement in unregistered provision, the incidence of which appears to have grown markedly in the last year'*.

I   Audit Commission survey of LEAs.

II   DfES, 2001. The rate of exclusion for pupils with statements was 0.3 per cent compared to 0.1 per cent for pupils without statements.

III   WAG, 2001. The rate of exclusion for pupils with statements was 0.6 per cent compared to 0.07 per cent for pupils without statements.

IV   In 2000/01, boys represented 83 per cent of permanent exclusions in England and 87 per cent in Wales.

V   See literature review, page 31.

VI   Audit Commission survey of LEAs.

Table 4

Permanent exclusions from maintained schools in 22 LEAs, 2000/01

Children with SEN account for the vast majority of permanent exclusions.

	Primary schools	Secondary schools	Special schools
Exclusions of children with statements	67	138	41
Exclusions of children with SEN without a statement	100	480	0
Total permanent exclusions (all children)	192	1023	41
Children with SEN as a percentage of all those permanently excluded	**87%**	**60%**	**100%**

Source: Audit Commission survey of LEAs (22 respondents)

73 **We recommend that national statistics should include a breakdown of permanent exclusions of children with SEN both with and without a statement. There should be further research into the link between SEN and school exclusions and the long-term implications for the young people involved.**

74 DfES draft guidance on school exclusions **(Ref. 10)** stresses that permanent exclusion should be used only as a last resort and that:

Other than in exceptional circumstances, schools should avoid permanently excluding pupils with statements ... Schools should try every practicable means to maintain placements, including seeking LEA and other professional advice where appropriate.

75 This is welcome, but given the high rate of permanent exclusions among children with SEN without statements revealed by local statistics and the fivefold variation in statementing rates between LEA areas, **we recommend that this condition should apply to all children with SEN, including those without a statement.**

76 **We also recommend that LEAs should develop the role of pupil referral units to provide short-term placements and outreach support to children at risk of exclusion.** This has been developed in Denbighshire and has resulted in earlier intervention and a fall in exclusion levels **[Case Study 4, overleaf]**.

Case study 4
Behavioural support in Denbighshire

Denbighshire LEA redeveloped its pupil referral unit to offer short-term, flexible placements to pupils at risk of exclusion. They did this in response to concerns that many young people were spending long periods in the PRU – and as a consequence, that growing numbers were having to receive home tuition.

They developed a six-week rolling programme, enabling young people to come out of school for respite and intensive support. Primary school children attend for half-day sessions only. At the end of this period, specialist teachers and learning support assistants from the PRU support their re-integration. Schools pay for provision in the PRU by the day.

The system was developed in consultation with local schools – on the understanding that they should be able to access short-term support more readily, but in return, they should be less ready to exclude pupils. Its success relies on the strong relationship between the behavioural support service (based at the PRU) and schools. Exclusions fell dramatically at first and, although they have since risen, a much lower rate of exclusion has been maintained. The LEA no longer issues statements for children with emotional behavioural difficulties (EBD), but supports children at School Action and School Action Plus. Only children with statements requiring special EBD provision (issued by other LEAs) now spend prolonged periods in the PRU, which does reduce the flexibility of the system.

Source: Audit Commission

Support in school

77 Children with SEN by definition need some form of 'additional or different' provision to make the most of their education. Our research suggests that how far this is delivered varies from school to school and area to area, even where it has been specified in a statement. It also reveals a mismatch between what parents expect and what schools feel that they are able to deliver, given the competing demands on their resources. This in part reflects a lack of clarity in SEN funding arrangements, discussed later in this chapter [paragraphs 88-89].

We got a mum helping out – how are they going to know about the national curriculum – they aren't teachers!

Father

I got her to the school that I wanted but in the last year she has learnt nothing apart from how to sit in the medical room. They have doubled her class size and so she is not getting the attention that she needs.

Mother

LEA advice and support

78 Local authorities have an important role to play in providing advice and support to schools, through educational psychology, learning and behavioural support services. SEN support services usually consist of teams of specialist teachers and other professionals who advise schools on effective strategies for working with children with particular needs. Arrangements vary greatly, as some LEAs have already delegated much of their funding to schools. Nonetheless, a number of common themes emerged from our research:

- **a strong sense of unmet demand** for specialist advice and support, across all types of setting and in all areas. This was most acute among early years providers, who appeared to have little if any systematic access to SEN support services or to the educational psychology service; and for children at School Action and School Action Plus, as resources were focused overwhelmingly on children with statements. By contrast, few SENCOs felt that there were shortfalls in LEA support for children with statements.[I]

- **concerns about the future of central SEN support services in the context of increased delegation of funding to schools.** In one area we visited, where most resources for learning support had been delegated, schools felt that the service was 'spread thinly' and excessive demands were being made of the specialist teachers now employed by individual schools. Several interviewees highlighted their concern about the continued viability of support services for children with low incidence needs, echoing concerns raised in other research **(Refs. 11 and 12)**.

- a feeling that **the distribution of the available resources was unfair** and did not reflect the profile of pupil needs in each school. For example, in one area, each primary school received the same allocation, regardless of its size or pupil needs, although there were plans to differentiate this in future; and

- **inadequate advice and support in minority languages and, in Wales, in Welsh.** Our survey showed that speech and language therapy and special school placements were only available in Welsh in a minority of Welsh LEAs. Other research has highlighted the scarcity of Welsh-speaking educational psychologists and shortages in Welsh-speaking SEN personnel and services **(Ref. 13)**.

79 It is perhaps inevitable that demand for advice and support on SEN will always outstrip supply and this makes it all the more important to make best use of the available resources. Earlier in this report we made a number of recommendations about early intervention [paragraph 39]. In addition to this, we recommend:

- **LEAs should allocate support from the educational psychology service and SEN support services to schools in the light of pupils' needs, including those at School Action and School Action Plus.** It is important that schools should understand how and for what purpose resources are distributed;

- **LEAs should carefully plan the ongoing role of central advisory and support services, in particular, for children with low incidence needs.**[II]

[I] Only 6 of the 41 SENCOs responding to our questionnaire felt that there were shortfalls in LEA services for children with statements. See also discussion on early intervention, paragraphs 34-38.

[II] We also recommend that this should be discussed at the Schools Forum, paragraph 91.

- **LEAs should explore the scope for developing local special schools (including non-maintained and independent schools) to provide advice and support to their mainstream counterparts;**

- **in areas with significant minority populations, LEAs should increase the availability of learning support and educational psychology services in minority languages** or, at the very least, ensure that adequate translation and interpreting facilities are available. **In Wales, LEAs should take steps to extend the availability of these services in Welsh.**

Support from health and social services

80 Many headteachers and SENCOs spoke of their difficulty in accessing advice and support from health and social services. Social services were widely perceived as being 'in crisis' and several interviewees reported that they would only respond to child protection cases. Shortages in health services were frequently highlighted, in particular, speech and language therapy. Several of the parents we interviewed said that the lack of such services lay behind their decision to send their child to a special school.[I]

81 This is consistent with evidence from our national survey of LEAs. Over four-fifths of respondents reported that aspects of health and social services provision were *'commonly unavailable or not available at all, despite being specified in a statement'*. Speech and language therapy was the most common shortage area, followed by occupational therapy and child and adolescent mental health services **[Exhibit 6]**.

82 'Joined-up' planning and provision poses a challenge to all local agencies and while we saw much evidence of considerable efforts being made to achieve this, progress was held back by differing spending priorities and boundaries, together with a lack of shared language and definitions across agencies. There were many positive examples of partnership working to meet the needs of very young children, often led by the Child Development Centre, but little evidence of successful joined-up working for children of school age. Few authorities appear to be taking advantage of Health Act flexibilities allowing them to pool budgets to support particular client groups.

83 It is clear that educational inclusion poses particular challenges to health and social services, as children with complex needs who might previously have been grouped together in special schools are increasingly attending local mainstream schools. Our research suggests that local agencies are having difficulty responding to this agenda. This requires action at both a local and national level. We recommend that:

- **LEAs actively consult colleagues in health and social services in developing their inclusion strategy; and**

- **the Department of Health and the Welsh Assembly Government establish clear expectations of the level of support and advice that health and social services should provide for children with SEN, in the context of policy on inclusion. This should be incorporated in the National Service Framework for Children, currently being developed by the Department of Health.[II]**

I The NAW Health and Social Services committee recently reviewed services for children with 'special health needs' **(Ref. 14)**. Their findings are consistent with our research.

II This will establish new national standards for health and social services for children, against which future progress may be monitored. The Government have also announced their intention to pilot Children's Trusts, intended to enable local agencies to work together in planning and delivering co-ordinated services for children and their families.

Exhibit 6

Shortfalls in health and social services for children with statements

Children with statements often do not get the support they are meant to from health and social services.

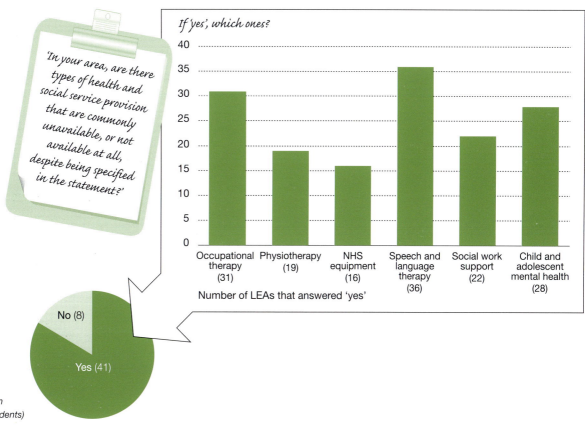

In your area, are there types of health and social service provision that are commonly unavailable, or not available at all, despite being specified in the statement?'

If 'yes', which ones?

No (8)

Yes (41)

Occupational therapy (31)
Physiotherapy (19)
NHS equipment (16)
Speech and language therapy (36)
Social work support (22)
Child and adolescent mental health (28)

Number of LEAs that answered 'yes'

Source: Audit Commission survey of LEAs (49 respondents)

84 We also recommend that **Government ensures that health and social services be held to account for their part in meeting children's SEN**. This may require a change to primary legislation: under the 1996 Education Act, health and social services are only required to provide support to children with statements in so far as their overall resources and priorities allow. Another option would be to ensure that children with SEN are accorded more priority as a client group; the National Service Framework for Children offers a unique opportunity to put this right. Unless children with SEN feature more prominently in the targets set for these services, it seems unlikely that this situation will improve.

I A range of approaches are used for distributing SEN resources to schools, for example, the number of pupils at School Action, School Action Plus and with statements; an audit of pupil needs; attainment data; and proxy indicators, such as free school meals. Each has its own advantages and disadvantages: this is discussed further in the LEA self-review handbook.

Box A

School funding for SEN

SEN funding has a number of elements...

- a proportion of the school's core budget ('pupil-led' or age weighted pupil unit – AWPU – funding);

- a sum delegated to meet the needs of children with SEN without a statement;

- a sum delegated to meet the needs of children with statements; and

- support from the LEA's SEN support services, either delegated as funding or as an allocation of hours.

Source: Audit Commission

Developing schools' capacity to meet children's needs

85 Inclusion is not – as some have suggested – 'SEN on the cheap'. On the contrary, if LEAs and schools are to fulfil their duties arising from the SEN and Disability Act 2001, there will need to be sustained investment in staff skills and school facilities. The final section of this chapter considers where schools and LEAs are and where they need to go in terms of resource management and staff skills.

Resource management

86 Resources – both human and financial – are a key determinant of how much support schools are able to offer individual pupils. Our research raises concerns about both the effectiveness of resource allocation by LEAs and schools' management of SEN resources.

Resource allocation to schools

87 Schools have a variety of sources of funding for children with SEN **[Box A]**. Funds are mostly allocated by the LEA, using a formula that aims to ensure a fair distribution. Formulae vary from area to area, taking into account factors such as pupil numbers and turnover, deprivation ratings and attainment data.[I]

88 Although some headteachers and SENCOs were broadly happy with the funding and support available to them, others expressed concerns about the way LEAs allocated resources for SEN:

- some **did not understand** the LEA's funding criteria for SEN or the delegation formula. This echoes a recent Ofsted report **(Ref. 9)** which found that *'funding formulae were too often over-complicated to the point of obscurity;'*

- some **disagreed** with the way resources were distributed to schools – for example, they felt that the proportion of children eligible for free school meals, a proxy indicator used in many areas, did not relate closely to the incidence of SEN; and

- some felt the amount of SEN resource available to their school was wholly **inadequate**.

89 A consistent theme across all areas was a **mismatch in school and LEA perceptions** as to what constituted their SEN budget. Headteachers typically viewed it as the funding they received over and above their base budget; however LEAs generally expected schools to spend a proportion of their core (AWPU) funding on SEN. This often results in disputes over who should meet the costs of additional provision. Schools typically told us that they spent above budget on SEN while others – including LEAs, local voluntary organisations and parents – suspected that schools sometimes used their SEN resources for other purposes. This lack of clarity undermines trust between all parties – and can mean that children do not receive the necessary support.

There's an obsession by (elected) members that we don't spend SEN money on SEN – but we subsidise our SEN allocation from our own budgets!

Headteacher

90 New education funding arrangements due to come into effect in April 2003 offer a unique opportunity to address these concerns. LEAs are required to establish Schools Forums made up of local headteachers and governors, which will advise on the way the schools' budget is allocated.[I] Regulations have yet to be published but it is envisaged that the Forums will:

- be consulted on the funding formula used to distribute resources between schools;

- give a 'schools' view' on policy issues that affect their funding, such as the inclusion of pupils with SEN into mainstream schools; and

- agree or impose conditions on the retention by the LEA of certain categories of expenditure **(Ref. 15)**.

91 An early task for the Schools Forum will be to consider how SEN resources are deployed. **We recommend that key issues for discussion should include:**

- **striking the right balance, in terms of maintaining central advisory and support services and delegating funding to schools;**

- **the delegation formula used to distribute resources to schools; and**

- **how far funding arrangements align with the agreed strategic approach:** for example, do they encourage early intervention?

92 Discussion at the Schools Forum could lead to much greater transparency in terms of the resources available for SEN, how they are distributed and, crucially, their expected purpose. This could provide a clearer basis for holding schools to account for their work on SEN – a key area for development in many areas, as discussed in Chapter four [paragraphs 110-112].[II]

School management of SEN

93 Two-thirds of SEN spending[III] is managed at school level and it is important that schools plan to make best use of their resources and be able to account for how they do so. The SEN co-ordinator (SENCO) plays a key role in the day-to-day management of SEN, but a number of concerns were raised about how effectively they were able to fulfil their role:

- Doubts were raised about whether SENCOs have **sufficient authority and influence** over school policy, decision-making and resource use. Our questionnaire indicated that more than two-fifths of SENCOs did not know the school's budget for SEN and a further one-fifth were only able to provide an estimate.[IV] In some of the schools we visited, such resourcing decisions were guarded by the headteacher.[V]

I Section 43, Education Act 2002.

II See also *Statutory Assessment and Statements of SEN: In Need of Review?*, paragraphs 39-45 and recommendations 1-3 **(Ref. 2)**.

III CIPFA education estimates 2001/02.

IV Audit Commission questionnaire of SENCOs in fieldwork LEAs.

V Note that in some schools – particularly small primary schools – the head teacher may fulfil the SENCO role.

- Doubts were also raised about SENCOs' **management capacity**. One in four SENCOs and over one-third of the headteachers we met felt the management time available for SEN in their school was 'inadequate' or 'totally inadequate'.[I] There was great variation in the time SENCOs were allowed for their SEN responsibilities – ranging from almost none due to a full teaching timetable, to being a full-time SENCO, with no teaching commitments. Some were managing large numbers of staff, for example, one was overseeing a department of 27 learning support assistants. Many reported that liaising with health and social services consumed a significant amount of their time. A minority had access to dedicated administrative support, allowing them to spend less time on the routine paperwork associated with SEN.

94 **We recommend that:**

- **Governing bodies and headteachers should ensure that the SENCO has:**
  - **sufficient 'non-contact time' for managing and planning SEN provision;**
  - **knowledge of the available resources for SEN and a say in how they are used;**
  - **sufficient authority within the school, possibly including a position on the senior leadership team; and**
  - **access to some administrative support.[II]**
- **LEAs should target SENCOs with training in the effective management of SEN – including resource management and record-keeping; and**
- **a national SENCO qualification should be developed to raise the status of this important role and to ensure that SENCOs have the necessary skills.**

Staff skills

Unless we develop the expertise in the schools, we can't progress inclusion… there's some excellent practice, but some abysmal practice.

LEA Head of Inclusion

Skills in mainstream classrooms

95 The more inclusive the classroom, the greater the diversity of needs among its pupils – and, in turn, the greater the challenge teachers face to tailor lessons to suit the aptitudes of each and every pupil. Many teachers feel under considerable pressure, on the one hand to meet the needs of individual pupils, and on the other to deliver a demanding national curriculum and achieve ever-better test results; research suggests that many feel ill-equipped for this task.[III] We interviewed over 40 SENCOs, many of whom felt their colleagues lacked confidence in working with children with SEN. They identified a number of training priorities for school staff **[Exhibit 7]**.

I As for above, plus Audit Commission questionnaire of headteachers in fieldwork LEAs.

II This builds on the recommendations set out in the SEN Code of Practice.

III See literature review, page 3.

Exhibit 7
Staff training priorities
The top priorities identified by SENCOs relate to core classroom skills.

Staff training needs	Priority
Curriculum differentiation	☆☆☆
Behaviour management	☆☆☆
Target-setting/writing and using IEPs*	☆☆☆
New SEN Code of Practice	☆☆☆
Teaching literacy	☆☆
Working with assistants/ inclusive classrooms	☆☆
Dyslexia/specific learning difficulties	☆☆
Identifying needs/early identification	☆☆
General understanding of SEN	☆
Speech and language difficulties	☆
Working with other agencies	☆

*Note: IEP is shorthand for individual education plan.
Source: *Audit Commission questionnaire of SENCOs (41 respondents)*

96 SENCOs' concerns were echoed by many of the parents we met, who were often disappointed at the level of SEN-related expertise in school. Some parents had clear – (at times, unrealistic) expectations of what was needed in terms of specialist skills or interventions, based on a range of information from newspaper articles, television programmes, internet searches and local voluntary organisations. Several commented more generally on some teachers' lack of understanding, particularly in relation to children with behavioural difficulties. Their perceptions are consistent with academic research which indicates that staff skills and confidence in relation to SEN vary widely.[I]

Even though they do training – a day or two here and there – they don't know enough. I expected the support assistant to know something about autism.

Mother

I See literature review, pages 3 and 32, in relation to behaviour.

My history teacher is horrible. I got spellings wrong and I now have to write them out ten times, 200 words – and I am dyslexic! I spoke to Mrs [SENCO] and she is trying to sort this out.

Pupil

Sometimes they just say he is naughty and send him home, but he is not – there is a lack of awareness.

Mother of child with attention deficit disorder

97 Developing the skills and thereby the confidence of staff in mainstream schools is fundamental to making inclusion work. This requires careful planning and action at all levels. We recommend that:

- **schools audit the SEN-related training needs of all their staff** and seek to ensure that they are addressed through continuing professional development opportunities.[I] This might be done most appropriately by departmental heads, as part of their wider consideration of the skills mix needed to deliver the curriculum. This should extend to non-teaching and supply staff, where relevant;

- **SEN-related training needs and training undertaken should be regularly reported to governors;**

- **LEAs should gather information on the training needs identified by schools and put in place a coherent programme of professional development opportunities.** At present there appears to be much variation in the availability of SEN-related training – schools in one area complained of an unco-ordinated array of courses, leaving headteachers to find independent providers to meet their requirements, while in another they spoke highly of the opportunities available; and

- **LEAs should seek to develop the training role of special schools where they have relevant expertise – both in terms of outreach work and on-site training – as well as fostering learning opportunities between mainstream and special schools** (see Case study 2, page 22).

98 At a national level, the new standards for qualified teacher status **(Ref. 5)**, which came into effect in September 2002, represent a step forward in many respects; the standard on curriculum differentiation is particularly welcome.[II] However, the standards fall short in their failure to reflect the wider policy context of inclusion. Although trainees are expected to learn about the SEN Code of Practice, it is surprising that there is no mention of the National Curriculum Inclusion Statement or, crucially, the Disability Discrimination Act. The latter includes important anti-discriminatory provisions, of which all staff should be aware. More generally, it is essential that trainee teachers should understand the value placed on helping children with SEN to acheive, including those who may be among the most challenging to teach; and that SEN is a core part of their teaching responsibilities, not an 'add-on'.

I   Schools may wish to make use of National SEN Specialist Standards published by the TTA **(Ref. 16)** which is an audit tool, designed to help schools to identify training needs in relation to pupils with higher levels of need.

II   Standard 3.3.4 states: *'They differentiate their teaching to meet the needs of pupils, including the more able and those with special educational needs. They may have guidance from an experienced teacher where appropriate.'*

Skills in the early years sector

99 A number of concerns were raised about the ability of early years providers to respond to children's needs, reflecting the relatively low levels of qualifications and pay and the high level of staff turnover in the sector. On a more positive note, others felt that the training many early years workers had in early child development provided a valuable background to working with children with SEN; and many suggested that the early years sector was more inclusive in its ethos than later stages of education.

100 In the last few years, the DfES has made available funding to increase skills levels in the early years sector. Targets have been set to:

- establish SENCOs in every registered early years setting;

- provide three days' training for each SENCO by 2004;

- establish 850 area SENCOs to support non-maintained settings, with at least one 'area SENCO' per 20 settings; and

- create a network of 'area specialists' to provide expert advice and support to SENCOs.[I]

101 These initiatives are welcome, but even so, specialist expertise will remain thinly spread among the plethora of small providers in the early years sector. **We recommend that LEAs should work in partnership with the EYDCP to ensure that relevant training opportunities are available to early years staff; and monitor the take-up of training across different sectors.**

Skills in special schools

102 Although special school staff may have much experience in working with children with particular needs, many have had little specific training. Several of the special schools we visited said they recruit generalists and train them once in post, reflecting the lack of the training courses for special school teachers nationally.[II]

103 Following concerns raised by interviewees, we carried out an analysis of the age of teachers in mainstream and special settings. This showed that special school staff are on average older than their mainstream counterparts, with a significant proportion nearing retirement, and few young staff are joining to replace them **[Exhibit 8, overleaf]**. This raises serious concerns about the sustainability of the special sector and the quality of provision within it, at a time when the needs of special school pupils are becoming increasingly complex and diverse.[III] **We recommend that Government considers what action is necessary to ensure an adequate supply of skilled staff for the special school sector. LEAs should also consider this as part of their strategy for ensuring the supply and quality of teachers in their area.**[IV]

I The WAG is also looking at the feasibility of increasing specialist support to the early years sector.

II Teachers of classes of pupils with hearing, visual or multi-sensory impairment are required to have an approved qualification but there are no such requirements for other categories of need.

III See paragraphs 53 and 54 for further discussion of the changing needs profile of special school pupils.

IV LEAs do not have a specific responsibility in this area, but many have developed strategies to support schools in recruiting and retaining staff.

Exhibit 8

Age profile of teachers in special and mainstream schools

Many special school teachers are approaching retirement, while few younger staff are joining.

Percentage of classroom teachers

—▲— Special schools
and PRUs

—○— Mainstream nursery,
primary and secondary

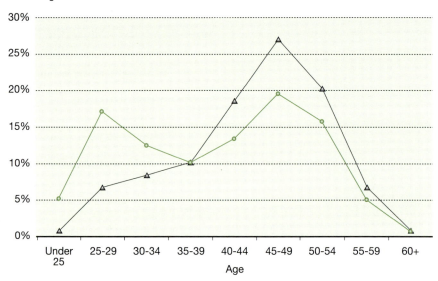

Age

Source: DfES, March 2000

4

Achievement

In contrast to the national focus on standards of attainment, little is known about the outcomes achieved by children with SEN. A lack of monitoring of their achievement and a lack of relevant performance measures make it difficult to recognise the good work in many schools, or to identify where children are poorly served.

Schools feel pulled in opposite directions by pressures to achieve ever-better academic results and to become more inclusive. National performance tables and targets fail to reflect the achievement of many children with SEN. Government needs to find a way of recognising and celebrating the achievements of these pupils and their teachers, often against considerable odds.

Monitoring and school 'self-review'

104 Both schools and LEAs have statutory duties to ensure that children's special educational needs are met and to promote high standards of achievement. This requires monitoring and review at a number of levels – the individual pupil, school and LEA.

Monitoring individual pupils – 'IEPs' and target setting

I would like to know how my son's progress compared with the rest of the class… but [the] school won't do this.

Mother

105 Schools are expected to set targets for all their pupils.[I] For most children with SEN, they also draw up an individual education plan (IEP), setting out targets relating to their needs. The SEN Code of Practice provides detailed guidance on the expected content of the IEP **[Box B]**.

Box B
Individual education plans

IEPs should be drawn up in consultation with the young person and his or her parents and reviewed at least twice a year. They should include:

• short-term targets for improvement covering key areas such as communication, literacy, numeracy, behaviour and social skills;

• provision to be made and teaching strategies to be used;

• when the plan will next be reviewed;

• success criteria; and

• outcomes – to be recorded when the IEP is reviewed.

Source: SEN Code of Practice **(Ref. 3)**

---

106 Although we did not specifically investigate the quality of IEPs, this emerged as an area of concern in our interviews with SENCOs, who identified target setting, writing and using IEPs among the top training needs of their colleagues. This echoes the findings of a 1999 Ofsted report which found: *'the writing and reviewing of IEPs is giving the greatest cause for concern to SENCOs in both primary and secondary schools.'* However, more recently Ofsted noted that *'the quality of assessment, recording and reporting is improving, and schools' use of this information in planning is becoming a strength rather than a common weakness'* **(Refs. 17 and 18)**.

107 The new standards for Qualified Teacher Status **(Ref. 5)** include a section on monitoring and assessment. While this provides a welcome starting-point, arguably this is a skill that may be best developed through practice and experience. **We therefore recommend that target-setting and assessment of pupils with SEN should be made a key area for development in the induction year.**[II] This could be achieved by working in partnership with other local schools, to make the most of their experience.

I Education Act, 1997.

II The TTA are currently reviewing the Induction Standards.

Monitoring by governors

108 Under the 1996 Education Act, school governors are required to *'use their best endeavours'* to ensure that children with SEN receive the provision they need. Furthermore, under the SEN Code of Practice **(Ref. 3)** they are expected to be *'up-to-date and knowledgeable about the school's SEN provision including how funding, equipment and personnel resources are deployed'* and to make sure that *'the quality of SEN provision is continually monitored'*. However, our interviews with governors – as well as with SENCOs, headteachers and LEA officers – suggest that monitoring by governors is very variable, depending on factors such as:

- their own skills, knowledge and experience of SEN;

- their own view of the appropriate balance of their role in terms of providing support and/or challenge – for example, pressing the LEA for more funds or questioning how the school had used the funds they had;

- their relationship with the headteacher; and

- the information they received on the performance of children with SEN and how SEN resources were being used.[I]

109 **We recommend that governors should request regular updates on the school's work on SEN, including the progress made by children with SEN, how resources are used and progress towards the School's Accessibility Plan.** Key areas about which governors – and in particular, the lead governor on SEN – should regularly enquire are set out in **Box C**. Given the varying expectations of both governors and headteachers, national guidance on this area could be valuable.

Box C
Questions for governors on SEN

Profile of pupils with SEN

- number of children at School Action, School Action Plus and with statements

- number of children with different types of need

- gender and ethnic profile of children with SEN

Staff skills

- when were SEN-related staff skills last reviewed?

- what were the outcomes of that review?

- what training has been undertaken?

Resources

- Resources available for SEN and how they are deployed – including:
    - core budget (pupil-led or AWPU funding);
    - funding for pupils with statements;
    - funding for pupils with SEN without statements; and
    - support in kind, for example, from the educational psychology service.

I See *Statutory Assessment and Statements of SEN: In Need of Review?*, paragraphs 43-45 and recommendation 2 **(Ref. 2)**.

Accessibility

- accessibility of school buildings, curriculum and printed materials and plans to extend this, as required by the SEN and Disability Act 2001

Outcomes

- academic attainment of pupils with SEN and progress made (or 'value added') over time;

- pupil and parental attendance at annual reviews;

- exclusions – permanent and fixed term – of pupils with SEN; and

- attendance of pupils with SEN – authorised and unauthorised.

Source: Audit Commission

Monitoring by LEAs

110 With resources for SEN increasingly being delegated to school level, it is critical that appropriate accountability structures are in place so that parents can be confident their child's needs are being met. Providing parents with this assurance is a key role for the LEA. This will become more important if fewer statements are to be issued in future, as appears to be the 'direction of travel' in many areas. Our survey found that barely one-half of local education authorities were systematically monitoring schools' work on SEN, although a third said that such systems were being developed **[Exhibit 9]**.[I]

I See *Statutory Assessment and Statements of SEN: In Need of Review?*, paragraphs 39-42 and recommendations 1-3 **(Ref. 2)**.

Exhibit 9

LEA monitoring of schools' performance on SEN

Barely half of LEAs are systematically monitoring schools' work on SEN.

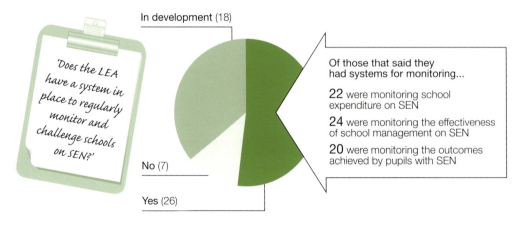

In development (18)

'Does the LEA have a system in place to regularly monitor and challenge schools on SEN?'

Of those that said they had systems for monitoring...

22 were monitoring school expenditure on SEN

24 were monitoring the effectiveness of school management on SEN

20 were monitoring the outcomes achieved by pupils with SEN

No (7)

Yes (26)

Source: Audit Commission survey of LEAs
(51 respondents)

111 We observed significant variation in accountability structures between areas, largely reflecting the historic relationship between the LEA and its schools. Several of the LEA officers interviewed doubted their ability to monitor schools' work on SEN more closely, because of the Code of Practice on LEA-School Relations **(Ref. 19)**. The Code emphasises 'intervention in inverse proportion to success' and, in this context, some authorities seemed unsure of their role in monitoring schools' performance on SEN, particularly with academically successful (but possibly less inclusive) schools.[I]

The LEA is aware, but it has no teeth with the schools.

Mother

School staff don't necessarily see the need to change because they have no big problems and the school's not in serious weaknesses or special measures.

Director of learning support

112 While many LEAs have well-established systems for monitoring school performance – often based on school self-review – inspection evidence indicates that SEN is often an underdeveloped element of such frameworks, and that there is a lack of clarity about where intervention should occur. **We recommend that all LEAs work with their schools to develop rigorous monitoring arrangements of their work on SEN – and in particular, systems for school 'supported self-review'.** Supported self-review involves a school reviewing its own performance within a framework agreed with the LEA. By using the same framework and a common set of criteria, schools are able to compare their performance against each other. This provides valuable information to the LEA about where they should target advice and support. The framework should also include clear 'triggers for intervention' to enable prompt and constructive action where problems occur **[Case study 5]**.[II]

Case study 5
School self-review in North Yorkshire

An LEA review 18 months ago identified inconsistencies in schools' accountability for their work on SEN, both in terms of reporting to governors and LEA monitoring, support and challenge. This was seen as a priority for development as the LEA is delegating more resources to schools from April 2003. The LEA developed a short self-review form (only two pages), asking schools to rate their own practice on a scale of one to three, against a range of criteria. These cover four key areas:

* the 'continuum of provision' for children with SEN, in particular in relation to literacy, numeracy and emotional and behavioural difficulties;

* management of SEN resources and accountability arrangements;

* assessment and monitoring of pupils' progress; and

* monitoring and evaluation by the SENCO.

Schools that complete the self-review and meet key criteria will be awarded an 'SEN Quality Mark' and receive Standards Fund grant for use with complete local discretion. Schools failing to meet the criteria receive support from the LEA to improve their provision, including more guided use of Standards Fund SEN allocations.

[I] However, the SEN Code of Practice **(Ref. 3)**, which takes precedent over the Code on LEA-School Relations, expects LEAs to publish their arrangements for 'auditing, planning, monitoring and reviewing provision for children with SEN (generally and in relation to individual pupils).'

[II] The Code of Practice on LEA-School relations **(Ref. 19)** emphasises the importance of establishing 'a clear process to identify early and support schools causing concern.'

The qualifying criteria will change over time to reflect new priorities for development. Validation visits will take place to evaluate the quality of responses.

Of all the schools in the area, 396 completed the review and only 11 did not. Feedback has been positive: most have said that they found it a useful exercise that has helped them to identify their own strengths and weaknesses. Schools are very pleased with the Quality Mark awards. The review forms one element of a wider framework for school self-review. LEA analysis of the information provided will be used to produce an annual report to governors, together with evidence from link advisers, the PPS, PLASC and annual reviews, and so on. It has also enabled the LEA to review its training programmes and to identify schools requiring support.

Source: Audit Commission

School improvement

113 A key element of school self-review should be a clear focus on pupil outcomes and how well children with SEN are being helped to achieve. Governing bodies have a duty to promote high standards of achievement under the School Standards and Framework Act 1998 and helping schools to improve their performance is also a key role for the LEA **(Ref. 20)**. In most areas this is achieved primarily through the LEA's inspection and advisory service (IAS) through occasional visits by link advisers and/or school improvement officers and the IAS may also prepare an annual 'school profile', providing a detailed breakdown of schools' performance. However, we found that there was often little sharing of expertise or information between the SEN function and the IAS. Separate analysis of the performance of pupils with SEN appeared to be generally underdeveloped.

114 Comparative information on the performance of pupils with similar levels of need, across different schools or over time, could throw light on which pupils are making good progress and which are falling behind. This could help schools to review their own practice and enable the LEA to target its advice and support more effectively. **We therefore recommend that LEAs should strengthen the links between their SEN and inspection and advisory functions, by:**

- **further developing link advisers' and school improvement officers' expertise in relation to SEN; and**

- **collecting and analysing data on the achievement of children with SEN, including those in special schools. This should form a key element of school self-review.**

Lack of relevant performance measures

115 One of the reasons why schools and LEAs have difficulty analysing the performance of children with SEN is a lack of national benchmarks – that is, expected standards of achievement – for many children with learning difficulties. This makes it hard to assess whether a child is making reasonable progress and to set suitably challenging targets.

116 Most children with SEN, including some children with higher levels of need, sit national tests and GCSE/GNVQs. However, a sizeable minority either do not sit such exams or do not gain any passes **[Table 5]**; few accepted measures exist for these children.

117 Progress has been made with the introduction of 'P-Scales' in England which measure the performance of children who are not expected to reach level two of the national curriculum. P-Scales were not introduced in Wales, although other systems are in use such as STEPS.[I] In addition, a number of LEAs have developed their own systems for measuring the attainment of children below national curriculum levels, such as Lancashire's PIVATS system (Performance Indicators for Value Added Target Setting), now used in a number of areas.

Every school is dreaming up their own systems... we would benefit from some exemplars of what others are doing.

Special school headteacher

118 However, many children fall between the two: even if they sit tests, they are unlikely to reach national norms because of their learning difficulty, but they are capable of achieving at standards well above those covered by the P-Scales. **We recommend that benchmarks should be developed for this sizeable group of pupils.**

Table 5
Pupils not entered for GCSEs/GNVQs or gaining no passes

Pupils in mainstream schools	England	Wales
not entered for any GCSEs or GNVQs	4%	6%
gaining no passes at GCSE or GNVQ	5.5%	7.9%
Pupils in special schools and PRUs		
not entered for any GCSEs or GNVQs	61%	94%
gaining no passes at GCSE or GNVQ	65%	94%
entry level qualifications	n/a	49% entered 44% gained a pass

Note: 'Entry level' is the first level of the national qualifications framework.

Source: DfES and WAG. Data relate to pupils aged 15 in 2000/01

I See also ACCAC, Practical suggestions for assessing pupils working towards level 1 **(Ref. 21)**.

119 The new pupil level annual schools census (PLASC) will collect information electronically on the performance of individual pupils and allow their progress to be tracked. From January 2003 in England and January 2004 in Wales, schools will be required to provide information on every pupil, including:

- whether he/she has a statement;

- whether he/she is at School Action, School Action Plus or School Action Plus and currently undergoing a statutory assessment; and

- from 2004, the nature of the pupil's needs.

This could in time yield valuable information on the performance of pupils with SEN, providing a basis for developing meaningful benchmarks.

120 **We also recommend that Government should explore ways in which pupils' achievements beyond the academic sphere, and the work of schools in promoting those achievements, could be recognised.** This could provide a more balanced picture of progress in relation to key lifeskills, such as communications skills, problem-solving, citizenship and aspects of personal, social and health education (PSHE).[I]

Inclusion and the standards agenda

There will be great opposition to inclusion until the issue of results is tackled.
Headteacher

121 Relatively little is known about the performance of children with SEN. Schools have difficulty setting targets and knowing what constitutes reasonable progress. Most LEAs are not monitoring outcomes for pupils with SEN or analysing their performance separately. And national performance targets – which focus overwhelmingly on the top 70-80 per cent of pupils – fail to reflect the achievements of children who have learning difficulties. Given the current drive to raise standards of attainment in schools, it is perhaps no surprise that children with SEN remain a low profile group.

122 This final section examines concerns about the perceived tension between the standards agenda and policy on inclusion. Almost every headteacher interviewed raised the issue of 'league tables' of school performance. This lay behind the reluctance of some to admit children with SEN, for fear they would 'drag down' the school's position; and could have a damaging impact on staff morale, failing to reflect the considerable achievements of some of the hardest-to-teach children and their teachers. This was seen as perhaps the key issue that the Government in England needed to address if committed to pursuing its policy of greater inclusion. It was perceived as less of an issue in Wales, where the Assembly Government has already ended the publication of national performance tables **(Ref. 21)**.

I   PSHE aims to equip young people with the skills and attitudes they will need to lead 'confident, healthy and responsible lives as individuals and members of society'.

I am all for inclusion, but when a child arrives with high levels of need my heart sinks… because we don't have the resources to support them and because of the effect on the SATs results.

Headteacher

SEN kids are included in the performance indicators, so they drag them down… they need to find ways to recognise what the school is achieving with kids with SEN.

Headteacher

We were lucky that he was able to sit his SATs as they said he would not be allowed to if his behaviour was not up to standard – and they didn't think he would get the grades.

Mother

123   Although this may in part reflect a long-standing opposition in some parts of the educational establishment to the publication of performance tables, there are genuine tensions which need to be addressed. Schools continue to be judged largely on the basis of the progress they make with children who do not have substantial learning difficulties, ie those who are capable of reaching national benchmarks such as 5 A*-C grades at GCSE. A school that is highly inclusive is likely, almost by definition, to have a higher proportion of pupils at the lower end of the attainment spectrum. It may therefore appear to perform poorly in a league table. Conversely, a school that is not welcoming to children with SEN may appear to be a 'good school' simply because it has fewer pupils with learning difficulties.

124   League tables do include measures of the number of children with statements and the number with SEN without a statement, but even these are crude indicators, given the great variation in practice. Moreover, SEN statistics seldom feature in national news coverage of the performance tables. Moves towards 'value-added' tables in both England and Wales are therefore welcome, as these will enable more meaningful judgements to be drawn about how a school has helped its pupils to progress. But even these may not do justice to the achievements of children with significant levels of need, whose progress may need to be measured in very small steps – and may perhaps only be compared meaningfully with children with similar levels of need. The DfES proposal to develop national benchmarking data based on the P-Scales is therefore welcome.[I]

I   The DfES plan to include a value-added measure in the secondary school tables from 2002 and in the primary school tables from 2003; these will show the progress made by pupils between key stage 3 and GCSE/GNVQ examinations and key stages 1 and 2 respectively. The WAG is also committed to supplementing local performance tables with value-added measures.

II   By 'inclusivity' we mean a school's commitment to working with children with SEN, reflected in all aspects of school policy and practice.

125   These developments may go some way towards addressing headteachers' concerns about national performance tables and their impact on inclusion. **We recommend that the Government should create new systems for recognising and celebrating schools' work with children who have SEN.** Three possibilities are:

- **A school's inclusivity[II] could be made a key dimension of school inspection judgements**, on a par with academic achievement. Currently a 'good' school is primarily one which achieves good results. A two-way matrix should be considered: a good school is a school that welcomes all pupils from the local community and achieves good results.

- **A school's inclusivity could be made a key criterion in assessing its eligibility for flagship initiatives**, such as beacon and specialist school status or 'earned autonomy'; and schools awarded such a status could be required to reserve a quota of places for children at the lower end of the attainment spectrum. This could go some way towards addressing popular concerns that moves to increase 'diversity' in secondary education will not benefit children with SEN.

- **Awards systems – at local and national level – could be developed to celebrate schools' work with children with SEN.** Some areas have developed local 'kitemarks' which recognise the achievement of individual schools on this front **[Case study 6]**.

Case Study 6
Celebrating inclusive schools in Manchester

The consultation on Manchester's SEN/Inclusion strategy revealed the tension felt by schools between the standards agenda and policy on inclusion. In response, the LEA is developing an inclusion kitemark to recognise and celebrate inclusive practice. A working group was set up to develop an easy-to-use but robust self-evaluation model. They drew on existing materials, including the Index for Inclusion, Ofsted guidance on *Evaluating Educational Inclusion* and the Healthy Schools Award, developing criteria and examples of evidence of inclusive practice.

Schools review their own practice and their judgements are moderated by their peers. The evidence is then validated by an external party, possibly the LEA. If successful, the school receives the 'Manchester Inclusion Award', which in future will be published alongside school performance tables. The award goes beyond SEN, also considering schools' work with minority groups and looked after children.

The award is being piloted and has been well received. Schools have welcomed the increased recognition of their work on SEN within the self-review framework. Following wider piloting, the LEA hopes to roll out the award in autumn 2003.

Source: Audit Commission

Conclusion

126 Our research has taken a wide-ranging look at how well the education system is serving children with SEN – and it reveals a picture of great variability. Whether and how children's needs are identified appears to be influenced by a range of factors, including their gender, ethnicity and family circumstances, where they live and which school they attend. This has implications for how much support they are offered. Most children with SEN are now educated in mainstream schools, although progress towards 'inclusion' has slowed down over the last decade. Some continue to face considerable barriers to learning, including inaccessible premises, unwelcoming attitudes, shortfalls in specialist support, and exclusion from aspects of school life. Children with SEN are more likely to be persistent non-attenders and to be permanently excluded. Very little is known about the educational attainment of children with SEN, or about how they fare beyond school.[I]

Time for a rethink?

127 Schools currently identify one in five children as having SEN and, for one in thirty, they consider they need additional external advice and/or support, provided through a statement. These are significant numbers and call into question how well our system of education is serving children whose needs differ in some way from their classmates'.

128 When a child is identified as having SEN a whole set of processes and structures come into operation. While these may be valuable in bringing a rigour to planning and possibly extra resources, they also imply a separateness that can be unhelpful. For example, the presence of a learning support assistant may mean that the class teacher gives less attention to a child with SEN; the statutory responsibilities of the LEA towards children with statements may allow individual schools to 'pass the buck' when problems occur; and at a national level, the interests of children with SEN may remain peripheral in mainstream policymaking.

129 Although many children with SEN require some additional support and a small minority need significant support, for the most part what they need is effective mainstream practice. Curriculum differentiation, target-setting for individual pupils and behavioural management are now expected of all teachers. 'Diversity' is the new vision for comprehensive education. In this context, arguably the time has come to rethink SEN: for real and sustainable improvements for this sizeable group of children may best be achieved by focusing on mainstream practice and, in particular, how our system of education responds to diversity. The debate now needs to move forward in a number of ways:

- from its current focus of 'picking up the pieces' for individual children, to responding to the diversity of needs in every classroom;

I   See literature review, pages 42-44.

- from a focus on paperwork, processes and inputs, to how each child is to be helped to progress and the outcomes they achieve;

- from a focus on what type of school children attend, to the quality of their experience there; and,

- from treating children with SEN as a peripheral interest in education policymaking, to putting them at the heart of mainstream policy and practice.

Refocusing SEN

130 Schools and LEAs have important new duties resulting from the SEN and Disability Act 2001 to increase their accessibility in the broadest terms and not to treat children with disabilities less favourably than their peers. This will require sustained investment in school facilities and staff skills as well as an attitudinal shift, so that children with SEN feel genuinely included in the life of their school. If successful, this could do much to remove the barriers to learning faced by many – which could in time allow for a refocusing of our system of special educational needs. Children with *'severe, complex and lifelong needs'* – for whom statements were initially envisaged[I] – would continue to benefit from special planning and support mechanisms; but there are many children for whom the SEN label might no longer be appropriate or necessary, as schools become more adept at responding to the diversity of needs in today's classrooms.

I The quotation is taken from the Warnock report, 1978 **(Ref. 24)**, which paved the way for the present statutory framework, leading to the 1981 Education Act, which introduced statements of SEN.

Recommendations

The report's recommendations aim to...

1 Promote consistent practice in identifying and meeting children's needs.

2 Promote early intervention.

3 Ensure that children with SEN are able to attend a local mainstream school, as far as possible.

4 Promote effective inter-agency planning and provision.

5 Enable children with SEN to join as fully as possible in the life of their school.

6 Develop the skills and confidence of staff to respond to the wide range of children's needs in classrooms today.

7 Promote the effective allocation and management of SEN resources.

8 Hold schools to account for their work on SEN.

9 Provide a more meaningful basis for monitoring schools' work on SEN.

10 Recognise schools' commitment to helping children with SEN to achieve.

1 To promote consistent practice in identifying and meeting children's needs...

Research should be carried out to investigate the significant gender differences in needs' identification and implications for how children's needs are met [para. 23].
DfES, WAG

The DfES and WAG should make available to LEAs data (from PLASC) on the ethnic background of pupils with SEN, to enable them to identify which groups are over- or under-represented [para. 26].
DfES, WAG

LEAs should ensure that appropriate translation and interpreting facilities are available for parents whose first language is not English [paras. 27; 79].
LEAs

Developing NQTs' skills and confidence at identifying SEN and making appropriate responses should be made a key element of the induction year [para. 33].
DfES, WAG

2 To promote early intervention...

LEAs should review their arrangements for funding SEN provision in early years settings, in consultation with the EYDCP, in particular, the availability of advice and support for children without statements and for those in non-maintained settings [para. 39].
LEAs, EYDCPs

Government should make available to LEAs funding to extend SEN advice and support to early years settings [para. 39].

DfES, WAG

LEAs should, in agreement with local schools, set targets to shift the balance of specialist advice and support towards 'whole school' and 'whole class' approaches [para. 39].

LEAs, Schools

3 To ensure that children with SEN are able to attend a local mainstream school, as far as possible...

LEA monitoring of school admissions should be discussed at least annually by the Local Admissions Forum, with a view to encouraging a more even distribution of children with SEN; it should include a separate analysis of admissions of children with behavioural difficulties [para. 46].

LEAs

LEA inclusion strategies should aim to ensure that all children may be educated locally, and as far as possible, in the mainstream sector. The strategy should be based on an analysis of pupil needs; establish a timetable for developing the capacity of mainstream schools and early years settings to meet a wider range of needs; set out clearly the future role of special schools; be underpinned by realistic financial planning and consistent with all other aspects of strategic and financial planning [paras. 20; 55; 56].

LEAs

The SEN and Disability Tribunal should reflect in its annual report on how far its decisions align with national policy on inclusion; and where, on the basis of the appeals it has heard, the key barriers to inclusion lie [para. 58].

SENDIST

4 To promote effective inter-agency planning and provision...

LEAs, health and social services should share information on children with complex needs, to enable sensitive forward planning [paras. 20; 39].

LEAs, Health, Social Services

LEAs should actively consult colleagues in health and social services in developing their inclusion strategy [para. 83].

LEAs

The DoH and the WAG should establish clear expectations of the level of support and advice that health and social services should provide for children with SEN, in the context of policy on inclusion. This should be incorporated in the National Service Framework for Children [para. 83].

DoH, WAG

Government should ensure that health and social services can be held to account for their part in meeting children's SEN; this should be reflected in the National Service Framework for Children [para. 84].

DoH, WAG

5 To enable children with SEN to join as fully as possible in the life of their school...

The WAG should evaluate the accessibility of school buildings and consider establishing a dedicated funding stream, similar to the Schools Access Initiative [para. 61].
WAG

Schools should record decisions not to include a child in any aspect of school life and report on this at their next review [para. 65].
Schools

When children with higher levels of need join a school, their class teacher (or other staff member) should develop an induction programme [para. 65].
Schools

Schools and, through them, LEAs, should collect attendance data on all pupils with SEN, both with and without statements [para. 68].
Schools, LEAs

LEAs should collect data on permanent exclusions of pupils with statements, by type of need [para. 70].
LEAs

National statistics on permanent exclusions should include a breakdown of permanent exclusions of children with SEN, both with and without statements [para. 73].
DfES, WAG

Research should be carried out into the link between SEN and school exclusions, and the long-term implications for the young people involved [para. 73].
DfES, WAG

Government guidance on school exclusions should emphasise that children with SEN – including those without statements – should not be excluded *'other than in exceptional circumstances'* [para. 75].
DfES, WAG

LEAs should develop the role of PRUs to provide short-term placements and outreach support to children with SEN who are at risk of exclusion [para. 76].
LEAs

LEAs should allocate support from the educational psychology service and SEN support services in the light of pupils' needs within each school, including those at School Action and School Action Plus [para. 79].
LEAs

LEAs should carefully plan the ongoing role of central advisory and support services, in particular for children with low incidence needs [para. 79].
LEAs

In areas with significant minority populations, LEAs should increase the availability of learning support and educational psychology services in minority languages or, at least ensure that adequate translation and interpreting facilities are available. In Wales, LEAs should take steps to extend the availability of these services in Welsh [para. 79].
LEAs

6 To develop the skills and confidence of staff to respond to the wide range of children's needs in classrooms today...

A national SENCO qualification should be developed to raise the status of the role and skill levels [para. 94].
DfES

Schools should audit the SEN-related training needs of all their staff and seek to ensure that they are addressed through continuing professional development. Action on this front should be regularly reported to governors [para. 97].
Schools

LEAs should gather information on the training needs identified by schools and put in place a coherent programme of professional development opportunities [para. 97].
LEAs

LEAs should seek to develop the training role of special schools where they have relevant expertise – both in terms of outreach work and on-site training – and foster learning opportunities between mainstream and special schools [paras. 79; 97].
LEAs

LEAs should work in partnership with the EYDCP to ensure that relevant training opportunities are available to early years staff and monitor the take-up of training across different sectors [para. 101].
LEAs, EYDCPs

Government should consider what action is necessary to ensure an adequate supply of suitably skilled staff for the special school sector [para. 103]. **DfES, WAG**

LEAs should consider what action is necessary to ensure an adequate supply of suitably skilled staff for the special school sector, as part of their strategy for ensuring the supply and quality of teachers in their area [para. 103].
LEAs

7 To promote the effective allocation and management of SEN resources...

Schools Forums should consider how SEN resources are deployed, in particular: striking the right balance in maintaining central support services and delegating funding to schools; the delegation formula used to distribute resources to schools; and how far funding arrangements align with the agreed strategic approach [para. 91].
LEAs, Schools

Governing bodies and headteachers should ensure that the SENCO has sufficient 'non-contact time'; knowledge of the available resources for SEN; sufficient authority to fulfil their role effectively; and access to some administrative support [para. 94].
Schools

LEAs should target SENCOs with training in the effective management of SEN – including resource management and record-keeping [para. 94].
LEAs

8 To hold schools to account for their work on SEN...

Target-setting and assessment of pupils with SEN should be made a key area for development in the induction year [para. 107].
DfES, WAG

Governors should request regular updates on the school's work on SEN, including the progress made by children with SEN, how resources are used and progress towards the school's Accessibility Plan [para. 109].
Schools

LEAs should work with their schools to develop rigorous monitoring arrangements of their work on SEN - and in particular, systems for 'supported self-review' [para. 112].
LEAs, Schools

9 To provide a more meaningful basis for monitoring schools' work on SEN...

LEAs should strengthen the links between their SEN and Inspection and Advisory functions, developing link advisers' and school improvement officers' expertise in relation to SEN; and analysing data on the achievement of children with SEN, including those in special schools [para. 114].
LEAs

National benchmarks should be developed for pupils who are unlikely to reach national norms because of their learning difficulty, but who are capable of achieving above the level of the P-Scales [para. 118].
DfES, WAG

Government should explore ways in which pupils' achievements beyond the academic sphere, and the work of schools in promoting those achievements, could be recognised [para. 120].
DfES, WAG

10 To recognise schools' commitment to helping children with SEN to achieve...

Government should create new systems for recognising and celebrating schools' work on SEN. This could involve school inspection judgements, eligibility for flagship initiatives and awards systems.
DfES, WAG

Appendix 1: overview of the statutory framework for SEN

The SEN framework

Arrangements for identifying and meeting special educational needs are set out in the 1996 Education Act, and before that, the 1993 and 1981 Education Acts. The 1996 Act was recently amended by the SEN and Disability Act 2001. Key provisions are summarised in the table below.

Section	Education Act 1996, Part IV
312	A child has SEN if he or she has a learning difficulty or disability which calls for provision which is 'additional or otherwise different from' the provision generally made for pupils of that age in local schools.
321	LEAs shall identify pupils who have SEN for whom they need to arrange special educational provision.
323	LEAs shall assess the needs of such children.
324	If the assessment shows that they require special provision to meet their needs, the LEA must 'make and maintain' a statement and arrange for the provision within it to be made.
317	Governing bodies must 'use their best endeavours' to ensure that children with SEN receive the support they need in school.

Under the 1996 Act, LEAs and school governing bodies must have regard to a statutory code of practice (**the SEN Code of Practice**) which sets out in detail how they are expected to carry out their duties. A new Code came into effect in 2002 and separate Codes apply in England and Wales. Key changes were to:

- replace the former four-stage process for meeting a child's needs with action at two levels – School Action and School Action Plus;

- place greater emphasis on the importance of involving parents and young people at every stage of the process;

- clarify the respective roles and responsibilities of schools and LEAs; and,

- promote effective working between agencies in planning and providing for children with SEN.

Inclusion

The SEN Green Paper (1997) **(Ref. 1)** emphasised the Government's commitment to developing greater inclusion – defined as follows:

'By inclusion we mean not only that pupils with SEN should wherever possible receive their education in a mainstream school, but that they should also join fully with their peers in the curriculum and life of the school.'

Subsequently, the SEN and Disability Act 2001 strengthened the right of children with SEN to attend a mainstream school, unless their parents choose otherwise or if this is incompatible with 'efficient education for other children' and there are no 'reasonable steps' which the school and LEA could take to prevent that. Other key aspects of the policy framework which promote inclusive practice are:

- the National Curriculum Inclusion Statement (DfES/QCA, 1999); and
- Evaluating Educational Inclusion (Ofsted, 2000).

Disability discrimination and improving accessibility

The SEN and Disability Act 2001 amends the Disability Discrimination Act 1995, placing important new duties on schools not to treat disabled pupils 'less favourably' than their peers and to make 'reasonable adjustments' for them. Specifically, they may not discriminate against disabled children in their admissions arrangements, in education and other activities (such as after school clubs, trips and orchestra) or by excluding them. A **Code of Practice for Schools (Ref. 25)** has been prepared by the Disability Rights Commission to help schools to implement their new duties.

The Act also requires LEAs and schools to plan strategically to increase the extent to which disabled pupils have full access to the curriculum and to school premises; and to improve the provision of written information in a form suited to pupil needs.[1] Schools are required to draw up and implement an Accessibility Plan and LEAs, an Accessibility Strategy. These will be inspected by Ofsted (England) and Estyn (Wales).

Working with parents

Under the SEN Code of Practice, schools and LEAs are expected to work closely with parents both in identifying children's needs and in involving them in decisions about their child's education. Under the 1996 Act, schools are required to inform parents where they are making special educational provision for their child. In addition, the SEN and Disability Act 2001 amends the 1996 Act, requiring LEAs to establish:

- parent-partnership services to offer impartial advice and support to parents on SEN matters. In many areas, these are contracted out to voluntary organisations; and
- disagreement resolution services, offering parents an 'early and informal' means of resolving any disputes they may have with the school or the LEA.

Appeals

Under the 1996 Education Act, parents have a right of appeal to the SEN Tribunal if they are not satisfied with the provision offered in a statement (including the school it names) or if the LEA refuses to carry out a statutory assessment, issue or maintain a statement. The SEN and Disability Act 2001 extended the Tribunal's remit to consider cases of disability discrimination in schools, so from September 2002, it became the SEN and Disability Tribunal. The Education Act 2002 provided for a separate Tribunal for Wales, with effect from September 2003.

[1] However, schools are not required to make physical alterations to their premises or to provide auxiliary aids (which it is envisaged, will continue to be provided for under the SEN framework).

Appendix 2: overview of responses to the *Policy Focus* paper

Our interim report, *Statutory Assessment and Statements of SEN: In Need of Review?* (June 2002) focused on the statutory framework for identifying and meeting children's needs – presenting evidence on both its shortcomings and its strengths **(Ref. 2)**. It made recommendations at two levels: action that schools and LEAs could take to meet children's needs more effectively within the current framework and the need for a high-level review of the statutory framework to consider options for future reform.

The report included a pull-out centrefold inviting feedback on its recommendations. Our thanks go to all those who responded. A total of 353 responses were received, reflecting a wide range of interests. The largest group of respondents were parents (32 per cent); followed by LEAs (28 per cent); schools (18 per cent); voluntary organisations (12 per cent); and health and social services (4 per cent).

Overall, there was strong support for the report's recommendations: all were supported by over 70 per cent of respondents, and nearly all by over 80 per cent.

The report's top recommendation was **'that Government should establish a high-level independent review to consider options for future reform – engaging all key stakeholders.'** Eighty per cent of respondents agreed with this, including 60 per cent who strongly agreed. Those who were most supportive were local education authorities, health and social services, teachers and national organisations (teacher unions and government); those who were least supportive were SENCOs, parents of children with statements and voluntary organisations.

Respondents were invited to identify key issues that should be addressed by the review. Key themes to emerge were:

* **collaboration and consensus** – in particular, the need for more joined-up working between agencies; more effort to engage meaningfully with parents; and the need to create a non-adversarial system, removing the tensions that currently exist between LEAs, schools and parents;

* **SEN funding** – many felt that SEN funding as a whole was inadequate;

* **accountability issues** – in particular, holding schools to account for their use of SEN funding; holding LEAs to account for fulfilling their statutory responsibilities towards children with statements; and holding other agencies to account for their part in meeting the needs of children with SEN;

* **staff skills and the availability of specialist advice** – including the recruitment and retention of SEN staff; the coverage of SEN in initial teacher training; and the availability of specialist central support services; and

- **assessment and needs' identification** – including the length and bureaucracy of statutory assessment; and the need to move towards more consistent ways of describing and responding to children's special educational needs.

A detailed analysis of the responses, carried out independently by the Institute of Education, London University, is available on the Commission's website at www.audit-commission.gov.uk.

Appendix 3: project advisory group

Gareth Adams	HMI, Estyn
Daryl Agnew	HMI, Ofsted
Maggie Angele	Education Consultant and Advisor (SEN)
Chris Beek	Capita Strategic Education Services
Mary Dickins	Independent Early Years Consultant
Alan Dyson	Special Needs Research Centre, University of Newcastle
Neil Fletcher	Head of Education, Local Government Association/ John Fowler, formerly Local Government Association
Kenny Frederick	Headteacher, George Green's School, Tower Hamlets
Ann Gross	Head of SEN Division, Department for Education and Sk
Sue Kerfoot	Head of SEN and Psychology Service, Essex LEA
Mary Kuhn	London SEN Regional Partnership
Suzanne Mackenzie	Principal Officer, National Union of Teachers
Alan Lansdown	Head of Pupil Support Division, National Assembly for V
Micheline Mason	Director, Alliance for Inclusive Education
Peter Meerstadt	Consultant Paediatrician, Greenwich Primary Care Trust
Philippa Russell	Director, Council for Disabled Children
Philippa Stobbs	Council for Disabled Children
Dave Tweddle	Senior Research Fellow, University of Manchester
Ruth Vincent	Director of Social Services, London Borough of Harrow
Chris Wells	Deputy Director of Education, Greenwich LEA
Mike Wilson	Assistant Director, West Sussex LEA and Chair of CONfED SEN Committee

Fieldwork sites

Short visits	**Full visits**
Camden	Denbighshire
Neath Port Talbot	Essex
Norfolk	Manchester
Sheffield	Newham
Tower Hamlets	Slough

References and acronyms

References

1 Department for Education and Employment, *Excellence for all children*, 1997 and Welsh Office, *The BEST for Special Education*, 1997.

2 Audit Commission, *Statutory Assessment and Statements of SEN: In Need of Review?*, Audit Commission, 2002.

3 Department for Education and Skills, *Special Educational Needs Code of Practice*, November 2001 and WAG, *Special Educational Needs Code of Practice*, February 2002.

4 Wedge and *Prosser, Born to Fail?*, National Children's Bureau, 1973.

5 Department for Education and Skills and Teacher Training Agency, *Qualifying to teach: professional standards for qualified teacher status and requirements for initial teacher training*, 2002.

6 HMSO, The SEN (Provision of Information by LEAs) (England) Regulations 2001.

7 SEN and Disability Tribunal, *Annual Report 2000-2001*, DfES December 2001.

8 Social Exclusion Unit, *Bridging the Gap: New Opportunities for 16-18 year olds not in Education, Employment or Training*, TSO, 1999.

9 Office for Standards in Education, *LEA Strategy for the Inclusion of Pupils with SEN*, 2002.

10 Department for Education and Skills, *Draft guidance on school exclusions*, 2002.

11 National Foundation for Educational Research, *Impact of Delegation on LEA Support Services for SEN*, November 1999.

12 Gray P., *Developing support for more inclusive schooling*, NASEN/DfES January 2001.

13 Roberts H., *Acknowledging Need*, Welsh Language Board 2002.

14 National Assembly for Wales, *Review of Services Children with Special Health Needs* (draft report), October 2002 (available from www.wales.gov.uk).

15 Education Funding Strategy Group, *Final Report*, 2002 (published on www.dfes.gov.uk).

16 Teacher Training Agency, *National SEN Specialist Standards*, December 1999.

17 Office for Standards in Education, *The SEN Code of Practice: three years on*, 1999.

18 Office for Standards in Education, *Standards and Quality in Education* (annual report), 2002.

19 Department for Education and Employment, *Code of Practice on LEA-School Relations*, 2001 and National Assembly for Wales, Code of Practice on LEA-School Relations, 2001.

20 Department for Education and Employment, *Role of the LEA in School Education*, October 2000.

21 ACCAC (Qualifications, Curriculum and Assessment Authority for Wales), *Practical Suggestions for Assessing Pupils Working Towards Level 1*, 1999.

22 National Assembly for Wales, *The Learning Country*, 2001.

23 Department for Education and Skills, *Publication of School and College Performance Tables in 2002*, March 2002.

24 *Special Educational Needs Report of the Committee of Enquiry into the Education of Handicapped Children and Young People*, HMSO 1978.

25 Disability Rights Commission, *Code of Practice for Schools*, DfES, 2002.

Acronyms used in this report

ASD	Autistic spectrum disorders
AWPU	Age-weighted pupil unit (pupil-led funding)
DfEE	Department for Education and Employment (now DfES)
DfES	Department for Education and Skills
DOH	Department of Health
EBD	Emotional and behavioural difficulties
Estyn	HMI for education and training in Wales
EYDCP	Early years development and childcare partnership
HMSO	Her Majesty's Stationery Office
LEA	Local education authority
MLD	Moderate learning difficulties
NASEN	National Association for Special Educational Needs
NAW	National Assembly for Wales (also WAG)
NCB	National Children's Bureau
NQT	Newly qualified teacher
ODPM	Office of the Deputy Prime Minister
Ofsted	Office for Standards in Education
PCT	Primary care trusts
PLASC	Pupil level annual schools census
PMLD	Profound and multiple learning difficulties
PRU	Pupil referral unit
PPS	Parent-Partnership Service
QCA	Qualifications and Curriculum Authority
SEN	Special educational needs
SENCO	SEN coordinator
SEU	Social exclusion unit
SLD	Severe learning difficulties
TSO	The Stationery Office
TTA	Teacher Training Agency
WAG	Welsh Assembly Government (also NAW)